POWER T

Also by Sue Smith

Romanian Rescue

Power to Parent

Rediscovering the miracle of family life

Sue Smith

Hodder & Stoughton

LONDON SYDNEY AUCKLAND

10 9 8 7 6 5 4 3 2 1

British Library Cataloguing in Publication Data
A record for this book is available from the British Library

ISBN 0 340 71016 0

Typeset by Avon Dataset Ltd, Bidford-on-Avon, Warks

Printed and bound in Great Britain by
Clays Ltd, St Ives plc

Hodder and Stoughton Ltd
A Division of Hodder Headline PLC
338 Euston Road
London NW1 3BH

To Simeon, Joel, Barnaby, Nathanael, Robert and most of all Graham, without whom this book could never have been written!

Contents

Thank You

There is always a danger that in thanking people for their help in producing a book, one will inadvertently miss someone out! So many people have encouraged me in the writing of *Power to Parent*, especially during crises of confidence over it! I am very grateful to them all. Special thanks also go to Nikki Griffiths, who faithfully read through the whole manuscript, pointing out grammatical errors and inconsistencies (and she's not even a parent!), and to Penny Atkinson, Heather Hughes and Jean Fish who acted as 'feedback' at several crucial stages. I am grateful to Suzanne Flint, of the Barbican bookshop, York, for her help in identifying resource materials, and to all the parents who filled in my questionnaire and contributed their significant insights. Thank you also to Rapport, for allowing me free use of their material.

Finally, thank you to my family for their wholehearted moral support, to Graham for his invaluable contribution at every level, and to my editor, Elspeth Taylor, for her practical help and sympathetic encouragement.

1

Power Cuts? Contact the Supplier

*My grace is sufficient for you, for my power is
made perfect in weakness.*
(2 Corinthians 12:9)

**Wanted! Full-Time Workers for the Most Important Job on
Earth!**
No qualifications required, but applicants must have a strong
commitment to the job, which is for life. They must be prepared to turn their hands to many skills: domestic management, first aid, conflict resolution, sewage and rubbish
disposal, catering, counselling, horticulture and childcare.
Knowledge of these and other skills not necessary, as
expertise is gained on the job, but ability to multi-task
essential. The job carries great responsibility, but no previous
experience required, nor references. No training, no on-the-
job support, no holidays, no sick leave, no bonuses. Salary:
nil – this is an altruistic vocation undertaken for love, with
definite but intangible returns. Other jobs may be taken in
addition to subsidise expenses, but no extra time will be
given for these.

Put like that, who would want the job? No one would believe
that it was possible to undertake. Yet millions of us already do
it! Parenthood fits the job description exactly, with many

additions not mentioned here, personally tailored to your lifestyle! Being a parent is indeed the most vital, significant, demanding and fulfilling job you will ever undertake. It never ends, even when the children are adults and no longer need your practical care, and in material terms it pays you nothing. In fact, it usually turns out to be an extremely expensive occupation!

Of course, the analogy breaks down after a while, because parenthood is so much more than just a job; it is an expression of love and giving. The innate, perhaps selfish urge in all of us to reproduce ourselves is also an opportunity to strive for higher ideals and 'make the world a better place' for and through our children. The most hardened, indifferent characters are moved, if only initially, by the instinct to care for and protect their children. Suddenly, we have a new purpose in life, a new responsibility, another person who is completely dependent on us for everything. It is a life-changing, soul-shaking, profoundly spiritual experience, and invariably brings out the best in us.

Paradoxically, parenthood can also bring out the worst in us. It is a condition of extremes! The continuing experience of having children opens you to the most intense range of emotions. You will feel joy and pure love such as you have never felt before, but you will also feel anger and frustration in equal intensity. Parenting pushes us to the limits of patience and endurance, but it also introduces us to realms of happiness which we didn't know existed. This apparent contradiction is quite hard to handle. How can something so wonderful produce, at times, such negative feelings? It has been said that being a parent teaches you as much about yourself as it does about children.

Throughout the writing of this book, I have had long discussions with many parents. I have also distributed a question-naire to a random group of friends, some parents from schools in York and Leeds, and church members of more than one church, finding out their views and feelings on every aspect of parenting. One of the issues which came over most clearly was the dual nature of the job. When asked what the two most overriding emotions of parenthood were, the majority of people gave two opposing answers, such as love and anxiety, joy and frustration, guilt and pleasure. This is the essential tension of parenthood; the positives and negatives battling in something fundamentally good, of God, are a reflection of life itself.

Handling the tension and allowing the positives to predominate is the challenge of parenthood. Most people want to be a good parent, and we all have high ideals when we embark on the exciting adventure. Here are some of the aims which the respondents to my questionnaire have for their children: that they are happy (by far the most popular aim); that they are healthy; that they become balanced, well-rounded adults; that they fulfil their potential; that they are successful in a career; that they feel loved and are loving; that they become responsible members of society; that they learn to love God for themselves. I'm sure that you can add further aims and ideals for your own children and family life. Sometimes they are not articulated, but are nonetheless there, part of your hopes and dreams for the future.

However, the physical, mental and emotional demands of bringing up children can take their toll, and there come times when life does not measure up to our ideals and then the guilt sets in. When you know what you want to achieve as a parent, but do not seem to be succeeding, discouragement and depression can result. The first time your delightful toddler screams 'no' and defies your instruction, or when previously loving sisters start quarrelling and making nasty remarks to each other, can be devastating. You have shown such love and care. Why are they behaving like this? Why aren't all those wonderful aims for my children being fulfilled? Why isn't having children up to my expectations?

A pervading sense of failure, sadly, underlies many parents' thinking and actions. Whenever their children do or say anything which does not line up with their aims and values for them, the parents believe the fault must lie with them. Some parents, unable to cope with such feelings, turn the blame on their children, and begin to resent them. The positives of parenthood then are submerged in anger, criticism and even, in extreme cases, abuse.

Sometimes, the demands of parenthood can seem too much. The need to be constantly giving, constantly putting others first, can prove too much of a challenge to that kernel of selfishness within us. Children are utterly dependent on us, and initially are not sensitive to our needs at all. I have to admit that it was not until I was a parent myself that I really appreciated all that my parents had done for me. As an older teenager and young adult I had been grateful and respectful to them (usually!) but still did not really comprehend all that bringing me up had entailed. Young children are blithely unaware of the demands they make on their parents, and while this is a natural state of affairs, it can sometimes breed resentment in overstretched adults.

An attitude of self-pity and exasperation results, with the consequence that time spent together with the children is not very fruitful or enjoyable. The children react to the underlying mood without understanding it and behave badly, thus confirming the parents' feelings about them. If this continues over a long period of time, rather than being a 'one-off', much harm can arise. Either the parents become permanently angry, overreacting to childish behaviour and speaking and acting towards their children in a damaging way, or else they become apathetic, not bothering to spend much quality time with their children, either letting them watch too much television and computer games, or else letting them 'play out' all the time, where they can get into all sorts of trouble. Obviously, any of these activities are fine in moderation, but too much, for wrong reasons, can become a problem.

I received a letter recently from a close friend who I know is a caring and involved mother. She has two boys, aged six and four, and was going through a difficult patch with her older boy, James. Her letter illustrates graphically some of the pressures of parenthood:

> I really need your help with how to deal with James. I feel like a complete failure with him. He is so difficult and I feel totally at a loss to know how to handle him.
>
> He comes back from school very grumpy, and even after food and relaxation is still really touchy. But even in the course of normal life, he is argumentative, goes crazy if he doesn't win, still often has paddies leaving people's houses, sometimes is aggressive towards other kids, hates it when things don't go his way, and still kicks against going to bed every night.
>
> We must have done something wrong way back in the beginning, though Philip [the younger son] does not seem as difficult – defiant, but not outrageous. James is so complex, because at other times he has such a sweet nature, is very gentle with the dog and visiting babies and says wonderful things about God. I don't understand. I don't understand him and I don't know how to deal with him. I feel, we both do, that we have used all sorts of different ways and that nothing seems to work.
>
> I felt, tonight, no love for him, just pure frustration. I feel like washing my hands of him and giving him to a foster parent who will probably be better and have more patience and more of an idea of how to deal with him.
>
> Please give me any ideas. I really do feel at my wits' end.

Does the rawness and honesty in this letter strike a chord? Needless to say, she did not 'wash her hands' of her child. Her love and commitment, and her *capability*, did she but know it, were far too great. This was not an inadequate mother, but one who was feeling the pressures of her responsibility very heavily at that point. In this, she is like so very many of us, who agonise over our children's behaviour and are worn out by their constant demands, who feel guilty about our impatience and losses of temper, who wish that we could be better parents.

In my questionnaire, I asked the participants to share some of the aspects of parenting which they found most demanding. Interestingly, one of the most frequent responses was tiredness. I can certainly identify with this occupational hazard! And it is difficult to maintain in yourself all the desirable qualities of parenthood when you are so tired that you can hardly keep your head up or even remember your name. Others spoke of the difficulty of being consistent in approach, while another recurring problem was trying to balance and answer the diversity of demands on time, emotions and energy. People noted discipline, responsibility, routine, arguments, wisdom in knowing how much freedom to allow, and 'being on call twenty-four hours a day, seven days a week', as all being demanding elements of parenting. Again, you could probably add many more to the list!

The good news is that we do not have to struggle alone with the challenges of parenthood. We do not have to feel guilty about 'the things we have done and the things we have left undone', for help is at hand; in fact, not in the form of a rescue mission but as an integral component of the whole parenthood package! God not only created parenthood, as part of his act of love towards mankind, but he also gave us the means to be successful in it. The Bible, his word to us, gives foundational principles for family life, and guidelines on how to bring children up. His Holy Spirit encourages and empowers us to act on those principles and guidelines, and gives us the wisdom to know what to do in specific situations. And through his Church he provides an extended family and support network so that we are not alone in this awesome task.

The paradox of parenthood generally is also evident in Christian parenthood. Some people might argue that a parent is a parent and that religious beliefs are not relevant – that what makes a parent is merely the physical fact of having children. At one level, this is undeniably true. However, parenting is more than a physical state, and there are as many different types of parent as there are types of person. Respondents to the questionnaire indicated that a strong spiritual belief did affect the way they parented. One third of the people who answered the questionnaires were Christian, others had some moral or spiritual belief system. Very few had no belief at all. In response to the question as to what ways their beliefs influenced their parenting, an interesting variety of answers were received.

Most people, whatever their belief, mentioned teaching children right from wrong, and giving them good values for the future. However, some people did not think their beliefs had any effect on their parenting at all, while a couple of parents actually thought that religious belief could have an adverse influence on the way their children were brought up. Perhaps thinking of situations like Northern Ireland or Israel, their opinion was that 'if people believe *too* strongly, it causes more damage than good'. Still on the negative side, one mum wrote that being a Christian actually made her more aware of her shortcomings as a parent. Others said that they would allow their children to make their own choices regarding religion when they were older, but would not direct them one way or the other.

Most people, though, were of the opinion that their religious or spiritual beliefs were a positive influence on their parenting. One respondent stated 'my faith helps me to cope with the low points', while another wrote that 'it helps to know that God understands my difficulties and forgives me when I am being really horrid'. Many people felt that being a Christian gave them a security in their parenting, and emphasised that they were inspired to set an example of faith, rather than lay down a set of religious rules. There was a general agreement that the Bible offered excellent principles for bringing up children and dealing with all the issues which arise in family life.

Being a Christian is not easy in a culture which increasingly dismisses and ridicules the faith. Many of God's ways and laws are now disregarded or openly flouted in society, and people who follow them are perceived as narrow-minded, simplistic or right-wing. Children in school are being taught theories (called facts) and principles which are in direct conflict with Christian teaching. The names of God and Jesus are constantly used as swear words, and blasphemy is offered as entertainment on television, film and in the theatre. As we attempt to *'bring [our children] up in the training and instruction of the Lord'* (Ephesians 6:1–4), we not only have to contend with all the inherent pressures of parenting, but we also have to battle against a culture which denies the validity or even the existence of God. The Christian viewpoint is marginalised or flatly contradicted, and Christian parents can sometimes feel besieged!

But *'the one who is in you is greater than the one who is in the world'* (1 John 4:4). We do not need to have a siege mentality, or grow paranoid, believing everyone is against us. We are not a tiny minority with our backs to the wall. Christianity is on the increase in this country, and world-wide it is growing at a phenomenal rate. The Christian magazine *Power for Living* points out that 'according to recent statistics more people have been born again since 1987 than in all of history put together! Viewed globally, the revival is on!' (*Power for Living*, Reapers Trust, Jan/Feb 1998). But even if that were not the case, *'if God is for us, who can be against us?'* (Romans 8:31). The verse is not an invitation to bury our heads in the sand and ignore the circumstances in which we live, but to acknowledge that, with God's power, we can succeed in them. Jesus came that we might have life and have it to the full (John 10:10) and that applies to family life as well! He wants us to enjoy ourselves as parents, and will help us to do so if we allow him. This is not triumphalism, but a realistic perception of the situation! Being a Christian parent is by no means an easy option, but it can still be fun and fulfilling.

Family life is in crisis as never before. One in three marriages in this country now end in divorce, and a huge number of children are born outside marriage. Lone parenting is on the increase, some of it by choice rather than necessity, and 'alternative' families are becoming the norm. Sharon, a friend of mine, came to me recently very upset about her sister, an unmarried mother with a seven-year-old son. Sharon had just discovered that her sister had begun a lesbian relationship with another single mother. The way she discovered? Her nephew told her, 'Mummy was lying underneath Mary, and their boobs were hanging out.' Shocked, she had confronted her sister, to have the story confirmed, although her sister had been unaware that the little boy had been watching. It's awful to think that such deviations from God's ways are becoming culturally acceptable. In some areas of the country, homosexual couples are now able to adopt children, which is mind-blowing when one considers how many other couples are refused on much less controversial grounds, such as age or race.

In our children's school, there are almost as many single-parent families as two-parent. The boys often talk in lowered tones of someone else's parents getting divorced. The other week, they came home with tales of a fight between Jason and Paul because Jason's mum had gone off with Paul's dad. Many of the children spend weekends in different houses, with the parent who lives away, and with whoever else happens to be living there at the time. Partners come and go, sometimes with other children attached, and the sense of confusion and insecurity grows. Often, the divorce is preceded by rows and emotional outbursts, and accompanied by much hostility and bitterness, which then lingers on in the aftermath of custody and access agreements.

Children are unwilling bystanders and participants in all of this unpleasantness, and it injures them at a fundamental level.

Even where a divorce has been conducted 'amicably' with minimum disruption to the children, they are still profoundly hurt by the whole affair. A friend of mine was six when his parents separated. Thirty years on, he can still vividly remember the experience, which they tried to make as gentle as possible. 'It felt as if my whole world was collapsing,' he says. 'My mum and dad didn't love each other, and they weren't going to live together any more. Home would never be the same again. I never knew where I belonged.' Another friend was a teenager when her parents divorced, but still felt that sense of devastation and loss. She also found it hard to trust herself in her own relationships with men. It was easier to have fun and move on, rather than risk commitment.

Teachers almost universally report a change for the worse in children's attitudes towards authority. There is a loss of respect for adults, a defiance in the way they approach them, which is deeply worrying. Children are prepared to challenge teachers now in a manner which would have been unimaginable only a few years ago. I have a friend who has just begun teaching in Wandsworth and is horrified at the behaviour of pupils there. She is a good teacher, enthusiastic about her subject, very caring about young people, but she has to spend most of each lesson just struggling to keep control. When she tells someone to stop doing something objectionable, or to leave the room, the response invariably is 'try and make me'. Even in primary schools, where I now do some supply teaching after years out of the system, one has to work harder to obtain obedience. Children have not been given boundaries and consistency at home, and so they are unable to cope with them at school. As the family breaks down, as parents either cannot or will not give their children the security and unconditional love they so desperately need, so a lost and hurting generation is growing up which in its turn will perpetuate the crisis.

In my capacity as governor of a local secondary school, I sometimes have to be present at disciplinary hearings for pupils who have gone through all other sanctions and are on the brink of being expelled. The case histories of these children are appalling, and make one realise again the danger that the family is in, and the damage that is being done to the children of broken and insecure homes. The 'system' does what it can to pick up the pieces, but often it is too late. What is needed is for the child to know that he is loved absolutely and that his home is safe and happy.

One child had been 'thrown out' of the home by her brutal stepfather and had to go into a Social Services flat at the age of sixteen. Her home environment had been one of violence and hate, and she found it impossible to control her temper, attacking anyone who crossed her and injuring one victim quite seriously. Her mother and stepfather didn't even bother to turn up to the meeting at school to discuss her future. It is highly probable that this damaged girl will herself have a child within the next few years, before she has sorted out her own problems, and then the whole vicious circle will turn again. The pattern of this story is all too familiar in our schools and social work files, and gives stark credence to the theory of a society in crisis.

God places great importance on the family. It is his blueprint for society. He models his Church, through which society will be transformed, on the family. Paul refers to God as '*the Father, from whom his whole family in heaven and on earth derives its name*' (Ephesians 3:15). Throughout the New Testament, there are many references to the Church as family, or more specifically to God as a father and Jesus as a son. He uses the image of the natural family to explain his own relationship with humankind; '*Which of you, if his son asks for bread, will give him a stone? Or if he asks for a fish, will give him a snake? If you, then, though you are evil, know how to give good gifts to your children, how much more will your Father in heaven give good gifts to those who ask him!*' (Matthew 7:9–11). The inference is clear; God created the family in his own image and he wants it extended to the Church and to the community. He used a family to bring his son to earth, and he will use families to bring him back again. The breakdown of the family in the twentieth century is symptomatic of that battle which is going on between the forces of good and evil.

As Christians, we have a mission not only to create the families he desires, but also to help reverse the disintegration of the family in society in general. The power he gives us to parent is not only for our own good, but to provide a model and a haven to those around us who do not yet have access to such power. We are a strategic part of a spiritual battle. Jesus won the ultimate victory when he died and rose again, but sporadic fighting continues and the enemy attacks wherever he sees God's plans in evidence.

It is not too fanciful, nor 'super-spiritual', to say that God wants to use us in our parenting to help overcome the evil which is attacking his creation. But he does not thrust us into this battle unarmed; *'The weapons we fight with are not the weapons of the world. On the contrary, they have divine power to demolish strongholds'* (2 Corinthians 10:4). These are not comfortable concepts to consider. It is simpler to confine ourselves to the legitimate concerns of practical care, discipline and how to balance all the various demands of family life. These issues, and many others, will be examined, but it is important also to bear in mind the wider purposes of our lives: God's 'hidden agenda' for our families!

How can anyone write a definitive book on parenting? How can I, I ask myself, as I gaze at a blank screen, or listen to my children squabbling, possibly tell other people how to do it? The answer, of course, is that I can't! Parenting is a unique experience for each person, and no one else could or should impose their opinions. It is also a very vulnerable state. Books, documentaries, leaflets, in fact anything or anyone with an air of authority, can make one feel extremely inadequate and 'condemned'. In the course of researching this book, I read a book which made me feel dreadful, because I was not doing half the things suggested by the author (who had four children, so I couldn't even use my usual, 'Well, it's OK for them, they've only got two children,' excuse!). I came away feeling that I could not possibly aspire to the near-perfect family life depicted in this book, and nearly handed in my resignation. I know that the author would not have wanted me to have such a reaction, and there were many useful ideas in the book, but nonetheless it was not helpful to me, because I felt that I compared very badly with the ideals portrayed. Of course, it is essential to have ideals, and it is not a good idea to compare yourself with others anyway, but it is also important to be aware that parents can be very fragile in their self-esteem, plagued by self-doubt and often anxious about the future.

Parenting is a unique experience, but there are also broad principles and skills which apply generally. Many of these are instinctive, but can still bear reiteration. Others require determination and effort to master. I have found it very valuable to spend time with people in a similar situation to my own, to share knowledge, advice and help about every issue to do with parenting. It is on such a basis that this book has been written. It is a means of sharing honestly the experiences and insights gained over the years from others and through many mistakes and failings. Though I have worked extensively with children in my job as a teacher and in the church, my only qualification for writing a book on parenting is that I am a parent! It is a sort of self-help manual, with ideas to encourage and provoke, but in no way to disapprove or dictate. Having children is wonderful and highly rewarding, but it is also demanding and very challenging at all levels. Parents need support, and encouragement that they are doing a good job. This book is in part an answer to that need.

It also aims to address some of the specifically Christian areas of parenting which are not usually covered in more general parenting books. As has already been mentioned, being a Christian and being a parent, and wanting the two to affect each other, raises a whole new set of questions and challenges.

My hope is that this book will help to focus many of the issues and inspire parents in their God-given responsibilities.

Since I could not have written a book about parenting without my children, I decided to make them integral to the very structure, to emphasise that I am writing as a peer not as a professional! When they were born, we chose names for them that had significant meanings. The names themselves are rather unusual, and drew cries of protest from grandparents each time, but what else can you do with a surname like Smith? I have used the meaning of each child's name to concentrate various ideas on the theme of parenting. Simeon means 'listening', Joel means 'the Lord is God', Barnaby means 'son of encouragement', Nathanael means 'gift of God'. Our fifth son, adopted from a Romanian orphanage, is called Robert, which means 'bright and famous'. This is not just a neat way to organise the chapters, but also intermingles the content and structure, rather in the manner that parenting itself does. The use of the male pronoun throughout the book might be thought to be a reflection of the fact that I only have sons and therefore favour that sex, but is in fact a grammatical contrivance, to avoid the clumsy 'his or her/he or she . . .' alternative.

Much is talked these days of 'parent power'. It is especially apparent in education, where parents now have much more influence in schools, supported by law. They have much more 'say' in the running of schools, and in the choices within the education system. Parents are also now a force to be reckoned with in political and commercial lobbying terms. There are many groups representing various parental interests which are vociferous and often successful in their efforts to change laws or company policies. I had a taste of my own parent power the other day when I had cause to write to a certain clothing retailer (which shall remain nameless!) because of poor service. I had a phone call in reply almost as soon as the letter dropped on to the manager's desk. He was most anxious to appease this mother of five, who represented not only a considerable amount of buying potential in her own right, but who could also influence a chunk of the next generation in their shopping habits!

Despite all this increased parent power, the wielders of it often feel extremely powerless, particularly within the bounds of their private family life! The aim of this book is to assist, encourage and envision parents in the amazing task they have been given, and to remind them of the power to parent which comes from the Lord, and not from their own, necessarily limited, resources.

Parenthood is God's invention, not only to secure the continuation of the human species, but to express his love for us and allow us to express his love for others. Even those who do not know him are demonstrating facets of his character when they love and nurture their offspring. We are all created in God's image, and part of that image is his parent heart. Therefore, it is natural, as well as supernatural, that we are able to draw on *his* power to parent.

2

A Gift For Life!
(Nathanael – Gift of God)

'Every good and perfect gift is from above, coming down from the Father of the heavenly lights, who does not change like shifting shadows.'
(James 1:17)

They had the future carefully mapped out. Mark and Rebecca were young professionals with demanding jobs, an attractive home and an affectionate dog. They would establish themselves in their careers and not succumb to the pressure to start a family too soon. Their spare time was taken up with the student group in the church, where they were popular and influential, and long walks in the countryside. Life was good and neither of them felt any particular urge to have children. Until, that is, some years later, when they finally decided that the time was right to begin a family. Somehow, it just did not seem to happen. At first they assumed that they were merely getting the timing wrong, but as month followed month with no tell-tale symptoms, they became concerned and finally visited the doctor for advice, astonished that they were unable to conceive as expected.

No one who has not experienced it can fully comprehend the prolonged agony of childlessness, the constant rollercoaster of emotions from desperate hope to bitter disappointment, the tense, tarnished lovemaking and the distance inexorably form- ing between two previously loving, understanding best friends. This is not the place to address the deep issues surrounding infertility, but what they do highlight is the truly miraculous aspect of conception. We should never take our ability to conceive for granted, even in these days of readily available family planning. The creation of a baby is still an act of God, however much of a hand we think we had in it. Mark and Rebecca believed that they were in control of how their family would develop, but found to their sorrow and pain that this was not the case. Now, after many years of trauma, frustration and difficulty, they have a lovely adopted son, whom they view as God's gift to them.

Conception, pregnancy and birth itself are acts of faith, ultimately out of our control. Not so many years ago, infant mortality before, during and after birth was quite common, and there was no assumption that all would necessarily go well. Nowadays, because of medical advances, having a baby is taken far more for granted, and infant deaths are, wonderfully, the exception rather than the rule. While we would never want a return to the era of annual pregnancies with almost half of them resulting in the baby's death, it would be no bad thing to be more aware of the fragility of the whole process. We can do all in our capability to assist, but in the end it is God who has the power of life and death. We can co-operate with him, but we cannot command, and the creation of new life should be viewed with wonder and humility.

That this life should be entrusted to us is even more amazing! A child is indeed a gift of God, not just the result of our planning (or lack of it!) and our mutual love. It is good to keep reminding ourselves of the fact, and to treasure our gifts at all times. My friend Cathy was amusingly reminded of this recently in an interchange with her oldest son, Tim.

Tim:	Are we going to have any more babies, Mummy?
Mummy:	No, not now. Mummy and Daddy are happy with their three boys.
Tim:	You never know, God might just send one.

Well, you never know!

Ready, steady, go!

Beginning a family might *feel* like the start of a marathon, but really it's just continuing the human race! A problem that many couples have is knowing when they are ready to begin. As soon as they contemplate the enormous, life-changing possibility of having a baby, a host of obstacles arise: 'We can't afford it yet', 'It's not a good point in my career', 'We want to finish doing up the house', 'We're not sure that we've had long enough as a couple', are frequently heard comments. Sometimes these are valid objections which must be taken into account, but the reality is that we will probably never feel completely ready for the responsibility of looking after another, totally dependent, human being.

It's not that the idea of a family is abhorrent, more that the accompanying responsibility feels too daunting. We feel inadequate for the job. But God understands this as he does all our other feelings, and I truly believe that he will make it clear when is the right time, if we ask him. As Christians, we can apply our principles of faith in this area as in all others, both about the timing and about the responsibility. Graham and I knew that we wanted children fairly quickly after marriage, as I was in my late twenties by then, but still felt a bit doubtful about the exact timing. As we prayed about it, we felt an increasing peace to go ahead without further delay. We planned to have a June baby, allowed a few months extra for possible 'near-misses' and ended up with a February baby!

Though in some ways we can never feel ready for what is to come, in others we can prepare ourselves a bit for the adventure of parenting. I find it quite ironic that in an age of ever more demanding qualifications, this most important job of all does not even require the most basic training. It is good to be as ready physically as possible, and this aspect will be covered in the following chapter. But we can also prepare ourselves mentally and spiritually as well. I am often teased for the number of books I will study before beginning a new project or new phase of life, and it is true that there is a danger in too much theory. However, I have found it so valuable to assimilate as much information as possible on the subject of childcare and child development. Unless our jobs are connected with children, the whole area can be shrouded in mystery, with only vague memories of our own childhood looming in the shadows. Reading round the subject can be useful in clarifying our thoughts, as long as we appreciate that reality and theory are often poles apart, and that we have not failed if we choose to ignore some of the advice in the books (except this one, of course!).

As far as it is possible, try to prepare mentally for the big adjustment life will require when a baby is part of the family. If both partners go out to work full time, it is possible that you will not know many people in the neighbourhood. It is worth beginning to get to know them before the baby arrives, so that when you stop paid work, there will be people you know to pass the time of day with. Many mothers have spoken of their sense of isolation and loneliness, marooned in a house with a tiny baby and with no one to talk to. The weeks and months immediately after having a baby are not the best ones to make new friends, so try and do it beforehand. It is worth visiting the local parent and toddler group while you are still pregnant and meeting others in the same situation before you have the baby. Then when you consider going after the baby is born, it will not seem such an ordeal.

When you have your first baby, you always assume that it will not make a huge difference to your lifestyle. 'Have baby, will travel' is the optimistic mentality, whether you intend to return to paid employment or work full-time with your child. It is true that there is no need to remain constantly in the house immersed in domesticity just because you have a child. It is undoubtedly good to get out with your baby if you can and do lots of things not necessarily connected with parenthood. When Simeon, our first child, was a tiny baby, I managed two classes at the local college, as well as some keep-fit and teaching English to an Asian lady in her house.

However, we delude ourselves if we think that the baby will fit round us, and it is as well to try and adjust to this big lifestyle change before it happens. Observe how people a stage or so ahead of you live, and imagine how this might apply to your own way of life. Most people cope well with the complete shift of focus in their lives, because they are besotted with their new baby, but the inability to call your time your own is more difficult to handle. Try and catch up on all those outstanding jobs, that pile of correspondence, those niggly DIY tasks, *before* the baby arrives, because, believe me, you will not have much time for them afterwards!

Preparing yourself spiritually for parenthood is quite difficult, because it is a unique spiritual experience and you don't know how it is going to feel! However, the more that you can pray about your impending parenthood and the child to come, the better it is. Lay hands on the 'bump' and pray aloud for the baby. They are responsive to the Spirit of God even in the womb! (An example of this was John the Baptist, who leaped in the womb as his mother was filled with the Spirit, Luke 1:41.) I liked to play worship tapes when I was able to rest in pregnancy, in the belief that the worship would somehow affect the baby. It is a proven fact that the unborn baby can hear sounds outside the womb, albeit filtered by the mother's body noises, and so it is not unreasonable to assume that the baby's spirit can also 'hear' from this early stage. We also played worship tapes, among others, during labour. This was primarily for our benefit, but I believe that they would have had a beneficial effect on the baby as well.

Parenthood, though a profound milestone on our spiritual journey, can also be spiritually draining, especially in the early days, and so it is a good idea to get your spiritual reserves high before the birth. A Bible study on children can be very helpful and encouraging, revealing God's perspective on what is about to happen to you, and giving you a firm foundation for your parenting. In our church, a few weeks before the due date, we have what is termed a 'baby shower', which is a lovely time of praying for mother and child. Everyone brings a small gift, something to eat and drink, and a prayer or prophecy. The mother-to-be opens the gifts, which are duly admired, we play some games related to babies or parenthood, and then we pray. Summarised thus, it sounds somewhat twee, but in actuality it can be a very special time of preparation. Sometimes the Lord brings a promise for the child or a word of encouragement, at other times there is an almost tangible awareness of his presence and his protection. It is very exciting, and provides an added security and peace as the birth approaches. Whether it is the first or fifth, it is good to feel as ready as possible for this new gift of life with which we have been entrusted.

'Surprise, surprise!'

It was April Fools' Day, and I thought I would play a joke on my mum. Seizing the advantage of the early morning, I rang her at about 8.30 a.m. and made my voice sound upset. She was concerned.

'Mum, I'm pregnant again.' There was a pause as she took in the implications, and then she rallied.

'Don't worry, you'll manage. You always wanted a big family.'

'Yes, but Joel's only four months old, and Simeon's only just two. What will I do?'

Mum was supportive, and I promised to ring back later, ending the conversation with 'April Fool!' and leaving her breathing revenge at the other end. However, she had the last laugh. Three months later, I was indeed pregnant unexpectedly (the result of 'natural' family planning!). And the due date? April 1st! Worse (or better!) still, my youngest sister's wedding was scheduled for April 2nd. My mother was torn between exasperation at such bad timing and satisfaction at the neat justice of it!

It is funny to look back on now, but at the time we were quite shocked. (In fact, appalled might better describe our initial reaction!) Joel, our second child, was still only seven months old, with Simeon at two years five months. I had not had very good pregnancies, and was still fairly exhausted. The thought of nine months more of nausea, with two tiny children to look after in addition, did not appeal at all. How would I manage with three children of three and under? How would I manage to get through the next few months? Would I get to Penny's wedding? How would she react to this unexpected hazard to her special day? (How would *you* feel if your sister was threatening to give birth as you floated down the aisle?) Could I handle the unavoidable barrage of funny comments from all our friends?

It was a fraught time, when we had to adjust to an in-evitability not of our deliberate making. It took a little while to come to a place of peace about the situation and to accept that God's timing is perfect and that this baby was as much his gift and in his purposes as the other two. We had always intended to have at least three children, so having another was not as much of a shock as it might have been; it was the timing of this one which was hard to come to terms with, plus, if we were honest, a faint sense of embarrassment at our now public inability to practise contraception correctly.

It was not a disaster, though, and within a short time we were tremendously excited at the prospect of another child. It would be lovely, I had convinced myself, to have them growing up so closely together. But the experience made me empathise with those who face an unexpected and perhaps unwanted pregnancy – that sense of panic and almost claustrophobia as one realises that events have spun out of control. Our 'surprise' was little more than that, but for some people a pregnancy could cause serious physical or mental damage. It might be the result of rape, and therefore repugnant, or might unbalance an already fragile mental or physical system. For many, an extra child could put an almost unbearable financial or emotional pressure on an already struggling family.

As Christians, we do not believe that abortion is an option, unless it is medical intervention to save life, but it is important that we approach the subject sensitively and be aware that such issues are always complex. There are women, it is true, who have abortions for purely social reasons and use it as a form of contraception, but there are many more who have a real struggle and who agonise long and hard before and after the event. These women need our support and help rather than our censure. God is forgiving towards those who are truly sorry for abortions they may have undergone or participated in. However, once life has been formed, the Bible tells us that it is for him only to sustain or take away. We need to deal with the consequences of 'accidents' within the will of God, the giver of life, not usurping his authority.

There are alternatives to abortion which stop short of taking life, and it would be good if society gave more emphasis to these. Adoption is a hard choice, but it is viable for those who really feel that they cannot cope with a child for whatever reason. There are thousands of childless couples who would welcome the opportunity to adopt one of these unwanted babies, whose barrenness is mocked and intensified by the needless deaths through abortion. There needs to be a financial incentive for mothers to keep their babies, and more support from counsellors and health visitors, so that people do not have to struggle alone in their parenting. Organisations such as Care for the Family who teach parenting skills require support so that they can extend their activities.

It seems old-fashioned in this amoral age, but educating teenagers that they do not *have* to have sex before marriage, that they can still enjoy life without it, and that they are not lacking or inadequate if they choose to wait, is one of the best answers to the burgeoning abortion and lone-parent problem in this nation. The only 'safe sex' is that which occurs within God's specifications, and this is being proved again and again, though it might not be expressed exactly in those words! Changing the culture of casual sex and the undermining of family life and positive values will take a miracle. But I believe in miracles, and I will do my best to help bring this one about. Will you?

Appreciate the gift!

'It's a boy! It's our Simeon! Oh, he's *beautiful*!' Graham's excited words were my first introduction to our first child, and I shall never forget the dazed wonder with which I gazed at this tiny product of our love. The joy and euphoria took a little longer to break through my physical discomfort and exhaustion, but the wonder and gratitude were there from the beginning. He was so perfect and yet so vulnerable, just beginning a life for which we were responsible. That sense of awe has been present at the birth of each of our children. Succeeding births are not diminished by familiarity. Each is a supernatural event in its own right, with its own powerful emotions. It is important that we don't lose sight of that wonder of the miracle of birth which we experienced at the beginning as the child grows older. There are many instances in our lives as parents when the frustrations and difficulties of parenthood overshadow the joy and wonder of it. It is important then to remind ourselves of the importance of the gift given to us by God, and not to devalue it by seeing only the challenges it has brought. Cultivate an attitude of thankfulness at *all* times – even the painful and frustrating ones!

Avoid negative talk

Either your own or other people's! There is a difference between honestly talking over a problem you may have in your parenting and constantly speaking negatively about your children. I have heard people describe their offspring as 'trouble' or 'little monster' as a matter of course, or employ words such as 'as usual', 'always', 'never' or 'I've had it up to here with them' when speaking of their behaviour. Any grouping of other parents, whether it be the toddler group or the crowd at the school gate, is seen as an opportunity to have a good moan about their children (and/or their partner).

It is too easy to slip into this way of speech, perceiving and dwelling on the problems your child presents, rather than the joys. Some people do not seem to enjoy their children, and warn you darkly about the next stage in your family life, which will inevitably be even worse than the present one. 'Wait till they're teenagers!' is a frequent offering, as is 'It doesn't get any easier, you know,' both said with furrowed brow and shaking of the head. At first, such words of encouragement used to make me quail (well, teenagers are scary, aren't they?!) but now I tend to ignore them, not because there are not grains of truth hidden there, but because I want to be thankful for my children and make the most of each stage of their development. I am not advocating boasting about one's child – a habit guaranteed to lose you friends – but rather, expressing the positive aspects of their character and behaviour. Try not to join in the critical talk around you, but instead counter it if possible (but sensitively, otherwise you and yours will be the next subject of the moan!).

It is indeed wonderful to be able to have children, and we should never take them for granted or lack gratitude for the gift we've been given. *'Sons are a heritage from the LORD, children a reward from him. Like arrows in the hands of a warrior are sons born in one's youth. Blessed is the man whose quiver is full of them'* (Psalm 127:3–5).

Don't see children as a limitation on your life, but as part of God's plan for you

Life pre- and post-children certainly is different! So different, in fact, that sometimes it is hard to believe that it was really you who used to curl up with a book and a cup of coffee in an evening, or who would spontaneously decide to go out to visit friends or to buy new clothes. Time, which used to be in fairly abundant supply, is suddenly on the endangered species list. Money likewise, as an infinite number of demands for it stretch away into the distant future. The close togetherness which you and your husband enjoyed will never be quite the same again. No more lazy Saturday mornings or leisurely walks through sun-drenched meadows, no more quick trips to the cinema or the shops. Such expeditions now have to be planned with almost military precision, and entail far more effort and thought.

In the hustle and bustle of everyday family life, it is tempting to look back in nostalgia to those days when children were a theoretical concept rather than an ever-present reality. Tempting also to notice the lifestyle limitations imposed by having children; the things which are impossible to do, the things which take five times longer to do, the loss of spontaneity, the impediment (or so it seems) to personal stimulation, spiritual development or career. It is possible to have feelings of resentment towards the children, particularly when they behave in especially childlike ways. Such feelings are understandable, but not particularly helpful.

It is more beneficial to readjust our whole thinking, and take on board God's vision for us as parents. If we accept the basic premise that it is in his plan for us to have children, then we can also accept that all his plans are for our best. To Jeremiah, he makes a statement which applies to us all: ' *"For I know the plans I have for you" declares the Lord, "plans to prosper you and not to harm you, plans to give you hope and a future" '* (Jeremiah 29:11). So having children is not a restriction to our lives but an expansion, an opening up of opportunities, a radical change for the better in the way we think and act. We are missing an important point if we define our parenthood in purely negative terms. Yes, some sacrifice of self is required, but the advantages of that far outweigh the disadvantages.

When the children were very small, and I seemed to have little time for much beyond feeding, changing and reading *Thomas the Tank Engine*, I used to think occasionally of my friend Sally, with whom I had reviewed the 'talent' (or lack of it) in our single days. She had remained single and done amazing things – a meteoric rise through schools to become a head, and then into positions of influence in the Education Department, writing books, leading worship at Christian conventions and preaching. I compared our careers to date, and the words 'cabbage' and 'vegetate' floated into my mind. She was doing all the things I might have done if circumstances had been different. But then I was reminded that although my achievements might not be so tangible, they are equally valid.

The lessons that we learn through parenting, the emotions we experience, the selflessness we can attain to, the opportunities opened up to us by this new lifestyle, the fun and adventure we can have, are all part of God's plan for us. It is our responsibility to enjoy it to the full, not complain about what we have had to give up. Sometimes we have to yield lesser dreams in order to fulfil the greater vision. I will probably not be a famous dancer or actress now (not that there was ever any likelihood of it outside my fantasies!), nor Director of Education, but I know fulfilment in every area of life. Though my career has not been conventionally successful, I am doing the jobs that God has given me to do to the best of my ability and enjoying them (most of the time!). I'm not sure that anyone could ask more of life or of the Lord.

And in the overall scheme of things, which God has in view all the time but which we rarely consider, our parenting has a place. God is building his kingdom here on earth, and your family, your children, have an important part to play in that. Sometimes we do not know ourselves how we influence other people, but as long as we are living God's way then we will do so. We need to keep our vision big, looking forward to opportunities and adventure rather than back with rose-tinted nostalgia.

Accept different standards without feeling inadequate

I can almost hear Graham's hollow laughter and charges of hypocrisy as I write this! I'm not fanatically houseproud, but I do like things in order, particularly, it has to be said, if we are having visitors.

'You wouldn't normally be doing this at this time,' he accuses me as we rush to get the children to bed before preparing a meal for friends.

I remove my head from the toilet to glare at him. 'I am *always* cleaning the toilet. How can you say I don't normally do this?'

'I said at *this* time. You don't usually clean when we're trying to put the children to bed. It's because people are coming. But they're not coming to see an immaculate house. They're coming to see us and have a good time.'

His logic is unanswerable, especially as he does an equal

share of the housework, but I cannot shake off the feeling that I am failing if the house is not always clean and tidy. I have theoretically high standards, and am constantly trying to live up to them. If people call in unexpectedly, which they frequently do, I am always pleased to see them but inevitably apologise for the state of the house. An element of this behaviour is, I am sorry to say, pride on my part. I cannot bear to be seen as an inadequate homemaker. I want to prove to all those doubters that I am able to cope with five boys, a husband who occasionally works away, leadership in the church, freelance writing, occasional teaching, school committees *and* keep the house pristine.

A common mindset is to see children as destroyers of a previous way of life and obstacles to regaining that way of life. We get frustrated because the house is a tip, and search desperately for moments when we can 'catch up with the housework'. Instead of spending time resting when the baby or toddler has a nap, we rush round trying to restore order and make the house look like it used to before children were on the agenda. We see the home as an extension of ourselves, and vow that having a child is not going to make any difference to standards of housework, cooking and social life. But it does. Sheila Bridge, in her admirable book *The Art of Plate Spinning* (Hodder and Stoughton, 1996), deals well with this particular issue. She says that her 'rule of thumb regarding housework deals with the problem of other people's standards as well as giving you a level to aim at. It is simply this: *Live in an environment which you control, not an environment which controls you.*' Different people have differing tolerance levels, and what is acceptable to one is not to another. An immaculate house with a frenzied owner is as tyrannical as a totally chaotic one where the essentials of life are lost beneath piles of washing, toys and rubbish.

There is a balance to this, as to every other aspect of parenting. We have to maintain standards of discipline, cleanliness and order to a level which will benefit the children and ourselves, but which is not unrealistically high. The same can apply to other standards which you had in a former life, such as cooking, cultural input and educational play. Rather than shrugging our shoulders in a defeatist fashion and feeling a failure, we should merely accept that standards are *different* with children, not necessarily lower. We can still cook fresh, healthy meals, but we cannot spend loving hours on multi-course cordon bleu confections. The house can be reasonably ordered and welcoming, but inevitably it will have that creative, 'lived-in' look! Of course, it is important to have a home that is comfortable and hygienic, but it will not be immaculate. It will be homely!

Try and get help to do those things which you feel are essential. Young people in the church are often happy to help out, and it is good training for them as well. If you can afford it, employ a cleaner. We had one when I was very ill, and though we struggled to pay her it was one of the best uses of money possible at the time. What bliss to come down to the smell of furniture polish and the sight of clean, tidy rooms! I'm sure it aided my recovery. Another idea is to contact local colleges to see if you are eligible for a nursery nurse or childcare placement. If you get a suitable student, it can be extremely beneficial for all concerned.

It's valuable to talk over your concerns with your spouse and devise a strategy for managing the home, rather than getting at each other when the state of the house depresses you totally! Hospitality will change as well, but it need not stop altogether. People are more ready than you are to accept a different way of doing things: open house, where people are welcome, but will probably end up holding a baby, playing a board game or washing up, casual meals, or coffee and nibbles instead of formal three-course dinners. In that way, you still have fellowship and stimulation without the strain of lengthy preparations.

Gifts are given to be enjoyed! This may sound somewhat

obvious, but it is possible to be so taken up with the responsibilities and stresses that the gift of children can entail that we
do not *positively* enjoy them. Each phase of the gift is so short
that if we do not make the most of it, we miss it. By focusing
chiefly on the challenges and possible negative effects of having
children, we can lose a vital element of parenting. Of course, no
one consciously focuses on the negatives, but, if we are honest,
we do not always appreciate and enjoy our gift as much as we
could. It is God's passionate desire that we take his joy in our
children and that we build that joy into them.

3

Guard your Gifts!

For God's gifts and his call are irrevocable.
(Romans 11:29)

It's not just when you arrive home from hospital for the first time with your tiny, precious bundle that the enormity of your responsibility comes upon you. At every milestone of their lives – starting primary school, starting secondary school, the first stay away from home, exams, the first 'grown-up' event without you, leaving home for college or a job – the sharp pang as you watch them go makes you realise again the vital part you play in their development. Of course, as they grow older, they learn to make their own choices, and we cannot be held accountable for decisions they make as adults, but we are foundational in their destiny.

With the gift of a child comes the call to care for him and bring him up in the ways of the Lord. God's word concerning Abraham is equally valid for all parents; *'For I have chosen him so that he will direct his children and his household after him to keep the way of the LORD by doing what is right and just, so that the LORD will bring about for Abraham what he has promised him'* (Genesis 18:19). It *is* an awesome responsibility, but with God's help it need not be overpowering.

Care for the gift

Practical care

There are many helpful and practical books on childcare, some of which are listed under 'Useful Resources', so I will not address the subject in depth here. However, it is worth reiterating the point that caring for yourself is an important aspect of caring for your children. Parents, and perhaps mothers in particular, are very prone to neglecting themselves in their efforts to look after the children. While ensuring that their children eat, sleep and exercise well, they do not take the same care about themselves. Usually, one is too tired or lacking in time to bother, but it is important to make the effort, otherwise the physical demands of life can become overwhelming.

Good health in pregnancy is vital in the development of a child throughout its life. If you can, begin before you are pregnant to prepare for the baby. Get fit – you're going to need to be! Lose weight if you need to, but don't overdo it. Eat a healthy diet and give up alcohol when you are attempting to conceive. Where possible, try not to put things into your body which might harm the baby. Probably a small amount of some things would be harmless, but if you can do without them, it is better to do so. I want to be able to look back, whatever happens to my children, and say that I did the very best I could to ensure their physical, mental and spiritual well-being. I don't want there to be shadows of doubt over any of my actions which could affect them in later life. Take plenty of rest and exercise, as well as eating a balanced diet and lots of extra vitamins and protein. Be guided by what your body feels and eat accordingly. Don't worry about getting fat; if your body needs extra carbohydrate, eat it! You can worry about getting rid of the extra pounds at a later date. Eating little and often (a habit I don't seem to have dropped!) can be helpful, especially if you feel, or are being, sick.

We found it valuable to go to ante-natal classes, such as those run by the NCT (National Childbirth Trust), and they gave us lots of advice about physical care as well as preparing for labour. Fathers too should look after themselves physically. They might not be undergoing the stresses of pregnancy and labour, but they still need to be fit for parenthood! A good idea is to try and build up good reserves of sleep before the arrival of each new baby: easier said than done, I know, but worth trying!

Just routine?

In the practical care of the child, it is valuable to have a long-term as well as an immediate approach. This particularly applies to the whole issue of routines. Some parents do not feel there is a need for regular patterns of behaviour. They want the child (and themselves) to be free of restrictions and to enjoy life together. They also feel that very young children are not able to understand, and that there is time enough to be restricted to time and routine when they are older.

I have sympathy with this theory, but it really is only a theory and rarely works well in practice. I have seen many children confused, tired and insecure because they are allowed to choose their own bedtime and to eat whenever they feel like it. Sometimes they are reprimanded for behaviour which is permitted on other days, sometimes they are bundled off to bed at an early hour, whereas there are other times when they are kept up until the small hours. Their bodies and minds cannot sustain a natural rhythm and they can become uncertain, low in self-esteem and even aggressive.

At the other extreme, though, I have seen routines practically made into a religion. When we visited Romania in the summer, we found that our friends Mihaela and Adrian were being ruled by a rigid system they had been set by 'professionals' as they struggled to look after their adopted twins. They would not deviate from the times allocated for sleeps and meals, even when we offered to take them out into the country, or for a meal. The twins were eighteen months old, and did not really need two hours' sleep in the morning and another two in the afternoon, but that is what Mihaela had been told, and that is how long they stayed in their cots while she tried to 'catch up' with household chores and meal preparations.

This was reminiscent of childcare teaching in Britain in the 1950s. While it is easy to denigrate it, there are useful lessons to learn. I too have felt anxious if I was not back at a certain time to get the baby to sleep or give him some lunch. The thought of a day out was too much to contemplate. Would snatched naps in the car ruin his sleep pattern for ever? Would he feed properly away from home? Silly fears, yes, but illustrative of the point that routines can control us if we are not careful.

Yet I do not believe that this is a good reason for abandoning them altogether. In the very early days, undoubtedly, it is almost impossible to get into a routine, and no sooner have you got into one than it changes. But after a few months, when you have got to know your new child a little, it is important to get into a routine, for the baby's sake as well as your own and any other children you may have. It is not easy, but if you persevere it does work, and will make life a lot easier for all concerned in the years to come.

A child needs the security of a regular, reasonably early bedtime, daytime naps and defined mealtimes to help him develop emotionally as well as physically. Obviously, as has been noted, there is no need to be rigid about routines, as there will be times when you will not be able to keep to them, but a general structure to the day will be very helpful. Babies quickly get the message about sleep times and will allow their bodies to get into a habit of sleeping at certain times if you let them. So there is no need always to wait until they are unbearably tired before putting them down. It is better to keep to a schedule whenever possible. Bedtimes should be calming, secure and relatively boring – not the time for Daddy to have a throwing up in the air and tickling session (or at least, not with the baby!).

A similar approach to meals is helpful. When children are tiny, feeding is on demand. There were some days when I seemed to have a baby permanently locked on to my breast. Every time I attempted some other activity, he would display unmistakable signs of hunger. But as they get older, and start on solids, it is possible to make mealtimes more structured. I appreciate that this is a very controversial aspect of parenting, and one where parents can easily feel inadequate and defensive. Children are actually quite manipulative little beings, and they rapidly learn to sense our vulnerable areas. They notice that we seem quite anxious to make them eat, and therefore work out that there is power in refusing food. I can identify with the school of thought that says that mealtimes must not become battle zones and that food should not be an issue of confrontation. Mealtimes should be enjoyable family times (do I hear hollow laughter again?!) and we should appreciate that children, like adults, have certain foods which they prefer to others.

However, I do not agree with giving in to children's food fads and allowing their fussiness to tyrannise the family and compromise their own health. I have heard of parents who cook two or three different main courses for each meal to cater for various likes and dislikes, and of children who will eat only a very narrow range of foods and who throw tantrums if asked to eat something they do not like. Now I know that there are some who will say, 'Let them eat what they like; they'll grow out of the faddiness, and at least they're eating *something* and we're not having rows at every mealtime.' I can see that point of view, and if it is something you believe strongly and it works, then go for it! But if you are not entirely happy with that strategy, then consider that it is not beneficial for a child to dictate his own way and that you are not doing him any favours in later life by giving in to him. Moreover, a restricted, usually 'junk' diet is not good for his general fitness, and may be detrimental to his health when he is an adult, if not before.

There are some tactics which may help to defuse the potentially explosive mealtime.

* Introduce your child to a wide range of savoury foods as early as possible, with a high content of fresh vegetables and fruit, bringing biscuits, sweets and other 'extras' into the diet as late as you can. This will help to bias the taste buds towards healthy savouries, and make the child open to trying new tastes.

* I have made it a general rule that the children do not eat between meals, although I'm a bit more relaxed about that now that they are older and have maintained huge appetites. If a child is constantly helping himself to snack food, he, naturally enough, will not feel like much to eat at mealtimes.

* If a child is hungry, he will eat. If he is reluctant, try to persuade, but if that does not work, then, without making a fuss, explain that there is nothing else on offer. If he wants, he can leave the table, but that there will be nothing else to eat until the next meal.

* Never offer an alternative. That way lies madness, especially if you have a large family!

* If your child really doesn't like something, give him a much reduced portion but insist that he eats a little of it. This is linked to a very real awareness of how fortunate we are to have food at all. Having spent time in poor and developing countries, I can't bear to see food wasted. It feels almost a crime to squander food when people are dying for want of it. (Cue for the usual riposte from disgruntled child, 'Well, put this in the post and send it to them, then.') Our children

have seen enough poverty to understand this concept, even though it doesn't always prevent them from objecting to certain foods when they are served up.

- Think ahead to their lives as older children and adults. There may be times when they are out somewhere and are offered food they do not like. I want them to be able to eat a little of what they do not like, in appreciation of the food and the person offering it. An example of this was in Romania, where the food is quite different. We were treated with loving hospitality by various friends, and the children eagerly ate what was offered, until meat was on the menu. I and two of the boys are vegetarian, and we always eat vegetarian at home. (The ultimate in fussy eating, some might think, but it is on principle rather than a matter of taste!) When our hosts were out of earshot, I explained that it was more important to honour them for their kindness and eat the food, rather than stick to principle. To have refused would have been to hurt or mortify them, and that was unthinkable. We did not find it easy, but we did it, and a valuable lesson was learnt! The ability to eat comprehensively starts very young. Many children will not even attempt some food because they have not been taught to try all sorts and to eat it without complaining.

Meals and eating generally can be fraught with tension, not least because they incorporate such high expectations. The image of the happy family sitting round the table, eating enthusiastically but impeccably, having a stimulating but courteous conversation, haunts me as I try to quiet the hubbub and prevent elbows jabbing next-door neighbours and mouths staying open when full of food. They are stressful times, especially if you have a fussy eater in the family, but don't give up! If you have instituted realistic routines and structures, it is worth persevering towards your ideal, because you will succeed eventually.

Emotional care

This is such a crucial topic, and again has been well covered by numerous other books. The Christian, though, has an additional perspective to consider when reading many of the secular books. Bringing up a child to be emotionally whole and confident is a hugely important job, and not at all simple. We bring our own insecurities and fears into parenthood, as we do into marriage, and these can be transmitted so easily to our children. Those character weaknesses and behaviour patterns that we are working on are suddenly revealed in glorious technicolour in our offspring, and we realise guiltily that we have reproduced aspects of ourselves which we would rather not have passed on.

But we can also impart all those positive emotions which we have received through our relationship with the Lord. Our nurturing of our children is an element of our expression of God's unconditional love for them. I still find such love a mind-blowing concept: that God loves me totally, passionately and forever, despite my failures, objectionable characteristics and striving to earn my way in; that he loves me purely for who I am, not for what I can do for him; that he loved me enough to sacrifice all for me. Once we have grasped the reality of that love, it transforms our whole way of life and thinking.

That is the love which we pour out on our children. Their initial experience of God, his care, compassion, comfort and authority, comes through us. And we must be unconditional in our loving. Many children feel that they are only loved and approved when they behave and achieve well. While we would vehemently deny that our love for them is based on their success, it is easy to convey, albeit inadvertently, that we love them more when they are 'good', or when they have achieved some success at school or in sport. The anxiety that many parents have for their children to do well can be translated by those children as an intolerance of any failure. They feel subconsciously that if they do not do well, they will lose their parents' love. So they then strive to earn their parents' approval and love, or else they rebel against them completely, choosing not to earn it at all.

The father's role in the emotional care of his children is critical. A child's perception of God as his Father is shaped by his relationship with his natural father. Many Christians' understanding of God as Father is distorted by inadequate relationships with their earthly fathers. This has certainly been my own experience. My father is a perfectionist, a clever, 'self-made' man with lots of drive and initiative. His work has always been of prime importance to him, though I do remember happy times in our childhood when he played with us or was the life and soul of birthday parties. But the very drive which has made him so successful in his work has made the critical aspect of his character predominate, and my sisters and I lived (and perhaps still do to a lesser extent) in fear of getting something wrong and triggering his wrath. He rarely praised but frequently criticised, so that we strove to please him out of fear and a desperate need to feel his love. When he was pleased, the sun shone and everyone felt warm, but it didn't happen very often. I cannot remember him ever telling me that he loved me.

When I became a Christian, my attitude towards God, although I didn't realise it, was coloured by my relationship with Dad. I wanted to please him, and if I failed, I felt that I had lost his love. I needed to be active in the church, because subconsciously I knew that by doing things I would please. I could not believe that I could be loved for who I was, but only for what I did. It required a revelation of God's love for me, combined with an ongoing healing of past hurts and wrong attitudes, to change my perception of my heavenly Father. Even now, though, I sometimes find myself reverting to those same old thought and behaviour patterns.

I have met many people like me whose relationships with

their fathers have impeded their relationship with God. I am sure that it is a key issue in parenting. I asked Graham for a father's insight on the subject:

So many men, particularly perhaps in the British culture, find it hard to communicate feelings and emotions. They are uncomfortable talking of deep issues, and prefer to cover over feelings with topical or flippant remarks. This book makes several references to showing children unconditional love. Fathers especially are prone to focus on their children's achievements. They give praise when their children do well in school or sport, but neglect to show appreciation for a positive character trait such as an act of kindness to a brother. Furthermore, they may fail to show love, just for its own sake. It is not only up to the child's mother to be physically demonstrative in affection, to use the words 'I love you', to take an interest in *their* world, all of which are vital for building up the child's emotional well-being.

While hugs and kisses and holding hands seem natural in a father's relationship with a young child, some find physical affection awkward as the son or daughter grows up. It need not cease altogether, even if it is expressed more in different forms of touch: a resting of hands on their shoulders while looking at the teenager's homework with them, an inter-locking of arms as you sit side by side to watch some television together.

A child also needs to know that his father is willing and able to give his full attention. After a stressful day at work and a tiring journey home, you don't always feel like con-centrating on the insistent demands of children delighted to see you back. But it is important to give undivided attention, if only for a short while, putting down whatever you are doing and making eye contact, so that your child knows you consider his needs, wants or interests to be of sufficient value for you to listen to him.

Every child, particularly in adolescence, also needs to know the respect of his father. This may sound somewhat strange, as normally the emphasis is on children respecting their parents. What I mean is that they should feel respected as individuals in their own right, and not just appendages to our lives. For example, it is a temptation to belittle their interests and tastes by mocking the incomprehensible din, which they dare to call music, blasting out of the loud-speakers. Perhaps Paul had the first-century equivalent of this in mind when he gave the exhortation, '*Fathers, do not exasperate your children*' (Ephesians 6:4). Giving them respect means that we should affirm them in their development as individuals with their own tastes and aspirations, which may increasingly differ from ours as they grow up.

No human relationship is going to be perfect but, with God's help, fathers can care for their children's emotions in such a way that they are secure in the love of their heavenly Father.

Channelling emotions

The wails reverberate through the house like wolves on a moonlit night. I rush upstairs, convinced that, this time, something truly terrible has happened. When I arrive in the bedroom, all I can see is Barnaby on his bed, in his favourite 'grief' position of head under the pillow and bottom in the air. No blood, no burglars, no battle; the bedroom looks as if it could have been the scene of one, but that is quite normal, I'm afraid!

'Whatever is the matter?' I ask, relief making me sound a little sharp. 'I thought someone was seriously hurt.'

'It's no good, I can't do it,' he says despairingly, indicating a complex wooden model he has been working on. 'I'm rubbish at it. And I don't like school, cos I'm rubbish at work too, and no one likes me, and . . .' This is from a boy who always has friends calling for him, who has excellent school reports, and who was happy and cheerful until about five minutes ago. We spend a long time talking and mending the model and trying to unravel and rationalise the complexities of our third child's volatile emotions.

It is important to allow children to express their feelings, but if you have scenes even remotely like the above, then you probably feel that far too much emotional expression goes on in your house! The skill comes in teaching them to channel those emotions in a creative way. Feelings which are allowed to run unchecked will eventually become destructive because they undermine self-control. Yet it is vital that we encourage our children to acknowledge deep feelings and to communicate them. It is in the communicating of them that we can teach them how to handle them.

Feelings themselves are neutral, they are neither good nor bad, they merely exist, as much a part of us as our physical make-up. But how we deal with those feelings is central to how we develop as mature adults. Being in touch with emotions can develop empathy, as long as the child is not allowed to be self-centred with emotions, so that they dominate his thinking. Long term, this will help him in future relationships, as well as helping you through the minefield of teenage angst.

So, how *do* you teach your toddler, who is throwing a tantrum in Tesco's, or your teenager, who is expressing his anger by being extremely rude, or your nine-year-old who is so excited by a forthcoming trip that she is wildly silly, to channel their emotions in a creative rather than a destructive way? Well, sometimes we don't. Sometimes we lose our temper, sometimes we shout or say things we shouldn't. Sometimes we smack in anger. In fact, we behave just like the children we are trying to teach.

If that happens, then the way we put things right is of crucial importance. Children have to learn that, unlike the Lord, we get it wrong sometimes. We need to ask forgiveness and explain why we became angry, so that the child realises that our behaviour was equally unacceptable. Otherwise, the inevitable times when we don't handle situations rightly will be imitated as a viable pattern by our children. But as John points out, *'if we confess our sins, [God] is faithful and just and will forgive us our sins and purify us from all unrighteousness'* (1 John 1:9). Having done that, we are free to address the issue which caused the crisis in the first place.

Often, a child in the grip of some extreme emotion, whether positive or negative, needs some time out to calm down before it can be discussed. Trying to channel his expression without that will only lead to confrontation and an escalation of the very emotions which you are attempting to guide. Make it clear, if appropriate, that the particular mode of expression is not acceptable, and firmly but gently withdraw him from the scene. At all costs, remain calm! Once a child has had some time and space to himself, in his bedroom, perhaps, or some other place where he can be alone and secure, then it is possible to talk quietly and meaningfully. I have had some of my most profound discussions with the children after some intense outburst of emotion. Despite everything, the incident, though painful at the time, has drawn us closer together, and given us a deeper understanding of each other's feelings and point of view.

Mental care

My mum used to tease me because we put books in Simeon's pram when he was a few months old, and used grown up words when we spoke to him rather than 'baby talk'. But though we undoubtedly were over-keen first parents, the principle still stands that it is never too early to stimulate children and encourage their intellectual development. Experiments have been carried out on rats (all books on childcare seem to have a reference to experiments on rats, so here is mine!) to show that the brain grows ever more complex in direct correlation to the amount of stimulation it receives. Those rats who were left in a boring cage with nothing to do except eat and sleep had very underdeveloped brains, whereas those who had been given lots of exciting activities and problem-solving toys with integrated rewards developed very advanced, complex brains. Though our children are not rats, we can apply the same principles to the area of their mental care.

With appropriate stimulation, we can aid our children's minds to achieve their full potential. This does not mean that we are teaching them to read at the age of two, or providing them with the very latest in computer hard- and software by the age of five. It does not necessarily cost a great deal to expose children to a wide range of stimulating, challenging experiences. It does require time, patience and some creativity. Talking to them all the time, even before they are able to understand, is important, though it can lead to embarrassing situations. A friend of ours was in the staffroom at work, having a coffee break, when someone dropped something. 'Ooh, bang!' he remarked automatically. 'Let's pick it up!' I have occasionally found myself talking to a supermarket trolley, having inadvertently mistaken it for a pushchair! However, don't let these dangers put you off talking to your offspring about anything and everything. Show them books and pictures, play lively games with them, and participate in interesting activities with them, whether they are two months, two years, twelve or sixteen. The need to stimulate them and encourage their mental processes never ceases.

It is important to take an interest in their school work (though, surprisingly, according to your child, he does 'nothing much' every day!). Look for things connected with topics or projects that they can take in, and support them in any work that they bring home. Listening to your child read every day is usually a required activity, but there are other ways as well that you can be involved in and help extend his schoolwork. When they get older, this becomes more challenging; we take an interest in our teenager's homework, and talk various aspects through with him when he needs it, but I'm afraid that much of it is beyond us already!

Be aware, though, of the danger of wanting your children to do well for your sake rather than theirs, and only desire that they fulfil their own potential, not your unrealistic expectations. As a teacher, I got used to anxious parents, convinced that their child was not doing as well as he should. A lot of the worry seemed to centre on the fact that little Johnny down the road was on a higher reading level, even though he was patently not as bright as their own child.

Children's self-esteem can be irreparably damaged if they feel that they are constantly disappointing their parents in ways in which they have no control. Just because you have a dream that your child will become the champion sportsman that you narrowly failed to be does not mean that he should be pushed beyond his abilities or desire. When we were in America, we were shocked at the fierce competitiveness we observed in Little League baseball games among the parents. They seemed far more involved and enthusiastic than the children, and we wondered for whose sake the game was being played. Such an attitude can slip into other areas, though, and it is important that a child is not put under undue pressure by the expectations of his parents.

Our aim is to give our children as many opportunities as possible to discover what they enjoy doing and what they shine at, and then to encourage them to do their best. Of course, in our heart of hearts, we want them to excel academically and be extremely talented to boot, but that is not very realistic, and we tell them that as long as they have done their best then we will be proud of them. And we are!

Make sure that their minds are as well fed as their bodies. 'Junk' food is fine occasionally as a treat, but not as a regular diet. Too much TV, unsuitable videos, overdosing on comics, heavy rock music, can all fill the mind with unhelpful images, impediments to healthy mental development. As parents we need, without getting too legalistic, to take responsibility for the kind of information, messages and attitudes our children's minds are receiving. As Christians, we have an external standard to work towards, besides our own instincts and opinions. The Bible does not have much to say specifically about television or comics, but its general principles, combined with the guidance of the Holy Spirit, will help us to make decisions.

Graham and I have always been quite strict about television use. The children are not allowed to turn it on without permission, and it only comes on for pre-chosen programmes, rather than being 'wallpaper'. They do not watch anything until early evening, except on special occasions, and they are not allowed to watch too much at a time. There have even been times, to my astonishment, when they have turned it off because they knew that I would not approve, and I wasn't on hand to consult. (There have also been times when the exact opposite has happened!) The rules also apply to the computer, which is in the family room so that children are not shut away alone for hours when using it. We make a distinction between educational software and pure games, and the latter are rationed: only two games per week, and only one per day as a spectator! It sounds a bit inflexible, but we have found that having a structure helps to keep a reasonable limit on what can become an addictive and essentially isolating activity.

Another way of aiding the development of your child's mental health is to keep in close touch with school, so that you are aware of the ethos and teaching there. Wield influence, if you have time, as a governor or member of the PTA, or go in as volunteer help. Teachers are on the same side as you, in wanting the best for your child, and will always discuss any concerns or worries you may have, if you express them in a non-threatening manner!

Spiritual care

One of our greatest responsibilities as parents is to nurture our children's spirits, to help them be sensitive to that element of life which is intangible, and which so many people ignore. As Christians, of course, we want them to grow up knowing and loving God for themselves, and accepting Jesus as their Lord, but beware the danger of imposing a faith on them. Our aim is that our homes and our own lives will reflect our beliefs, and the children will grow up in that environment of spirituality with a natural awareness of God and Jesus. In Deuteronomy, the Lord urges us to make children aware of him in their everyday lives: '*Teach [God's ways] to your children, talking about them as you sit at home and when you walk along the road, when you lie down and when you get up. Write them on the door frames of your houses and on your gates, so that your days and the days of your children may be many in the land . . .*' (Deuteronomy 11:19–21).

In our house, we are not super-spiritual. The children have the normal ups and downs and the same interests as any children, and as a family we do many things that any normal family would do. But we do talk about God in our everyday conversations, and it is natural for us to pray about things. Sometimes, the prayer is not answered straight away and we have to talk about that. Sometimes we forget to pray about things altogether, and, sadly, sometimes the Lord is not reflected in our lives, but generally his presence is acknowledged and celebrated in our home and we attempt to live according to his principles. Church meetings are fun and anticipated with enthusiasm, and the life of the church is very much intertwined with the life of the family.

But care for their spirits also means protecting those spirits from anything that might harm them, including crushing or repressing them with indoctrination. We cannot and should not impose a set of religious rules on our children, making them 'odd' and vulnerable among their peer group. Instead, we should help them to know God, to appreciate the eternal elements of life and the deep values of people rather than the materialism and egotism which pervades most of society. Enabling your child to have his own sincere and significant relationship with Jesus, a relationship of joy, love and fun which will stand against the pressures of the world and motivate him to care for others, is one of the most important things you will ever do in the whole of your life. This whole vital aspect of parenting will be discussed in greater depth in Chapters 4 and 5.

Celebrate the gift!

Gifts are usually given to celebrate an event or to express love at a special time. The gift of children is a cause for festivity at any time, even if there are some moments when we do not feel at all like celebrating. It is valuable to try and cultivate a sense of occasion and 'specialness' in the most mundane of activities. This really helps to raise the importance of family life, in the eyes of both the parents and the children, and helps to make the most of the time that they have together.

Children can be fun!

In fact, one of their main aims in life (besides the apparent one of driving their parents slowly insane) is to enjoy themselves. The trick is to enter into that enjoyment rather than view it as intrusive silliness or trivial childishness. Too often, even when we are present and not engaged in other activities, we watch or direct or applaud, rather than join in.

This came home to me very clearly when we were on holiday in the summer. We had stayed for a few days near the head-quarters of Graham's company near Cologne, and he had gone off to work, looking rather silly walking out of the campsite in a suit! The rest of us went for a walk in some lovely nearby woods, and after a while the children decided to play Billy 123, a variation of hide and seek. I watched and made sure that the younger ones had grasped the basics of the game, and encouraged them all as they played it. After a while, though, I realised that I was being a bit boring really, and decided to join in. When they realised that Mummy was hiding too, the boys were absolutely delighted, and the game took on an added zest. Months later, the boys still refer to the fun they had playing Billy 123 'with Mum joining in as well'. Joel commented that it was more fun when I played too. Of course, as they get older, they would be horrified if you joined in their activities (worse, you may be horrified if you *knew* their activities!) but they still want you to be actively involved in their lives.

It is vital to 'let our hair down' now and then and do ridiculous things, just to be part of the children's lives. Strangely enough, it is those absurd moments that they will remember into adulthood. For instance, we have a silly occasional tradition of making mundane domestic matters into a song, with everyone joining in. A boy cannot find a clean pair of pants in the morning, and begins to sing, 'I've got a pants problem, pants problem.' Gradually, others join in, harmonising (after a fashion!), ad libbing and with movements to match, so that the end result is like something from a variety show! It is hilarious, ridiculous and would lose us all cred if anyone were to see us, but it makes us laugh and gives us identity as a family. So ignore all the dreaded chores sometimes and sit down to watch an entertaining programme together, or join in a 'rough and tumble' rather than using that time as an opportunity to 'get on'.

Play games with them, tell jokes (if you have the stomach for it). You don't have to spend a lot of money to have fun; a walk in the countryside, a junk-modelling session, a 'bop' to your teenager's Big Mix '98 (within the privacy of your own home, and with curtains closed, of course!), a face painting or make-up attempt, water fights in the garden, or a family story-telling session. Even chores can be made amusing, if we have the time and energy to make them so. Certainly, if we make an effort to initiate the table-laying race or the vacuuming rodeo, it makes necessary jobs more resentment-free as well as more enjoyable. Children are naturally optimistic and fun-loving, and with a little thought it is possible to make most things positive for them. The ability to join in ourselves whenever possible will significantly enrich our family life.

Investing in memory banks

This is closely linked to having fun, as we want our children's memories to be positive and enjoyable. As children grow older, they will amass a series of highlights or low points which will be stored away in their memory bank, to be recalled, deliberately or by chance, in future years. The contents of your child's 'account' will directly affect their mental, spiritual and even physical well-being. How many of us, as adults, still have very clear snatches of memory from childhood? And how many of us are still affected, if only briefly, by negative memories? Sometimes, we are unaware that we have these images, until a crisis or circumstance recalls them. I have seen a young woman weeping in a communication workshop because she could not bring to mind one happy memory from childhood to share with her husband. I have known a grown man reduced to tears as something during the church meeting reminded him of his parents' unhappy marriage and his own feelings of fear and despair at the time. God can and does heal such painful memories, and offers a fresh start free from the past, but how much better if those memories did not exist in the first place.

As parents, our goal is to invest strong, positive memories into our children, so that they are built up in their own self-esteem and confidence and we are knit closer together as a family. Shared experiences are a great bonding agent. Again, it is not necessarily the most expensive activities (like buying shoes!) which are the most memorable. Sometimes, certainly, an expensive, much anticipated treat, like a trip to a theme park or an exciting holiday, can be a wonderful, lasting memory, but equally the day spent digging up and rearranging the garden to make an enclosure for the rabbit and the guinea-pig will go into the memory banks for ever. The memories become a treasure trove of shared joys and pleasures which form part of the child's security and identity as he ventures into adulthood.

Honouring your children

Gifts are normally treated with reverence (out of respect for the giver), gratitude and delight in the gift itself. To cast aside a gift or to belittle it is an insult to the giver and a rejection of the motivation behind the gift. We need to remember this precept in our attitude towards our children. In the midst of their bad attitudes, their defiant behaviour and their exhausting demands, they still need to be treated with honour as the precious gifts that they are. To honour someone is to give them a high place in your esteem, to praise and affirm them publicly as well as privately, to make them aware of the importance that you accord them in your life. Some people may think that this would be too difficult for a child to handle, making them spoilt, arrogant or precocious, but if the honouring is part of a whole attitude towards them which includes firm, loving discipline and well-defined boundaries, then it can only be beneficial.

It is also good for children to honour each other. A good way to encourage children to say good things about each other is in a slightly formalised family-time setting. We adapt what is known as 'circle time' at school, when the person who holds the special object (a small toy or ornament or even a spoon!)

holds the floor. So for the purposes of honouring each other, the theme would be, 'One thing I really like about . . . is . . .' The object is then passed on to the next person in the circle. This works remarkably well, even though the context is somewhat artificial. We also encourage the boys to say positive things about each other in the course of their everyday lives, and to speak up for each other. (This is not always as successful, though, unfortunately!)

- It is important always to give credit where it is due, even within the context of wrongdoing; for instance, a child hurts a sibling in anger, but takes responsibility for it, rather than lying as he has done in the past. In that situation, it is important that the child is praised for not lying and for owning up, even though he will still be disciplined for the original crime.

- Honour their achievements: frame certificates, put up pictures, tell grandparents about good school reports (you can boast to grandparents as to no other!), go to watch them play/dance/sing and if you can't get there, delegate someone else to be there. All these actions, which can sometimes seem a little tedious or trivial to us, are of vital importance to our children, for they demonstrate how much we value them.

- Try not to adopt negative thought and speech patterns about the children, even if they are driving you crazy! As has already been mentioned in Chapter 2, it is one thing to talk honestly with a friend or professional about aspects of parenthood which concern or defeat you, but another to have a negative mindset about them and undermine them to others, especially if it is within their hearing. Without wanting to be one of those tiresome mothers who can see no wrong in their children and who constantly boast of their latest achievement or cute saying, there is nothing wrong with being positive and appreciative of them, while acknowledging their weaker areas.

To know that you are honoured and valued is a basic human need and, as with other fundamentals of human development, must be built into your self-awareness from an early age. If this is achieved, then your child will be enabled to grow into confident, whole, secure adulthood.

4

God's in Charge – or is He?
(Joel – 'The Lord is God')

Blessed are all who fear the LORD, who walk in his ways ... Your
wife will be like a fruitful vine within your house; your sons will be
like olive shoots round your table.
Psalm 128:1,3

Picture the scene; an hour in the life of a 'normal' Christian family. You wake up with a headache, due to sleep deprivation. Do you immediately start humming choruses as you spring out of bed, or do you groan and turn over to try and snatch a few more moments' sleep? The children come bounding or drifting in, according to mood, and immediately begin squabbling about who can get into bed with you. Do you smile patiently and remind them that it is not loving to talk to each other like that, or do you irritably tell them all to get out of the bed and get dressed? The headache, predictably, has got worse by now. Do you spend some minutes with your husband, praying that God will heal it, or do you reach for the paracetamol? Time's running late, and there are still the dreaded packed lunches to make. The children do not seem to have a sense of urgency about this, and are engaged in a heated discussion about the now pop group. Do you round off the discussion with a few well-chosen words of your own about the pop group in question and then suggest a quick time of family prayer to start the day well, or do you raise your voice and tell them in no uncertain terms to hurry up and clear the table while they're about it?

Eventually, after finding lost PE kits, mending broken shoelaces and paying out huge amounts of money for school trips, visiting puppet shows and the like, you set off for school. Having waved them off with a smile of encouragement, do you return with a song of praise on your lips, ready for the next stage in your exciting day, or stagger in, heading straight for the kettle?

An exaggerated scene, of course, and not intended to resemble any real person, whether living or dead! Yet there are elements in it which can make all of us a little uncomfortable, and focus us on the question of just how much God really is Lord in our families. As Christians, we would not dispute the centrality of God's support and guidance in the bringing up of our children. However, practice often falls behind theory, no matter how hard we try. In turn, this makes us feel guilty and inadequate and the vicious circle starts to rotate again. Personally, I find it a lot easier to apply godly principles in the area of child-rearing when the children are not there!

There is a hard balance to strike between the 'super-spiritual' approach, where children are restricted by almost legalistic religious parameters, and the 'laid-back' approach, where almost anything goes, because God is love and, yes, we believe, but there's nothing wrong with being in the world as well. I have seen the results of the former approach, where children were made to feel guilty for childish irresponsibility and emotions, and where a highly charged atmosphere of pseudo-spirituality was often present in the parents. Their motives were right, but they laid too many of their own spiritual frustrations and expectations on their children, and did not fully allow them to behave as children. The youngsters are now in their teens, and have, hopefully only for the time being, rejected the Lord completely.

At the other end of the scale, though, are those families who, though Christian, hardly ever give God a look in. We have students in the church who come from homes like that, and they are confused, not knowing exactly what their relationship is with the Lord, in a sort of spiritual limbo. Their lifestyle is indistinguishable from non-believers', because either they do not really know God's ways, or else they do not really want to follow them. How can we get the balance right so that our children grow up as poised, truly whole beings, loving God, serving him and wanting him to be central in their lives? Perhaps it is easier if we consider how the Lord is God in different, related areas of our existence and how that will contribute to achieving the lordship of God in our parenting.

Lord in our individual lives

They will not learn what we do not live

We can – and sometimes do – teach what we do not live, but our children will not retain those lessons. The old adage of 'don't do what I do, do what I say' does not hold water, for children, inveterate imitators, will learn by what we do, whatever we say. In the short term they may accept what we say, even if they don't see it in our lives, but long term, which is where we are aiming in our parenting, they will perceive and reject the hypocrisy.

Before everyone sinks under a sea of self-condemnation, remembering all the dreadful gaps between God's ways and ours, it is vital to bear in mind that God accepts us as we are, and forgives and forgets our mistakes when we are truly sorry. To admit wrong and ask forgiveness is part of God's plan for us (1 John 1:9) and if our children see this aspect at work in us and imitate it, then they are learning valuable lessons about the Lord which will be foundational in their walk with him.

The key is our inner attitude towards God; do we long to know and serve him more, or is a relationship with him peripheral in our thoughts and actions, a Sunday activity, squeezed into a busy lifestyle almost out of habit or guilt? God longs for us with a passion beyond any human emotion, and a relationship with us is his great joy; that is what he created us for. Our own relationship with him will influence significantly our ability to parent as God desires.

Keep your fuel reserves topped up!

Being a parent is one of the most exacting jobs in existence, partly because of the huge responsibilities it carries and partly because it is twenty four hours a day. So it is easy and under-standable to 'run dry' occasionally, physically, mentally and spiritually. The three affect each other, so that if you are physically exhausted, it is more difficult to remain spiritually alert and 'on top'. Sometimes it is too much effort even to open the Bible or pray. When that happens, or when you are feeling too guilty or frustrated to communicate effectively with the Lord, these suggestions may help:

- Listen to worship tapes (preferably with feet up and eyes closed!) Even if you unintentionally drift off to sleep, your spirit will still be nourished, and the peace will do you untold good.

- Read a Christian magazine. They usually give inspiring teaching in 'bite size' pieces.

- Go for a walk, with or without offspring, and use it to clear your thoughts and give thanks to God for all his benefits. The exercise and change of scene will improve your perspective on life, and you will inevitably see or think of things for which to thank God.

- Have a conversation with God about anything and everything, as if he were a friend round for coffee.

- Sit in absolute silence for a while (even if it's on the toilet!) and allow God to speak to you.

- Spend time with Christian friends who will encourage you.

- Don't go on the crèche rota at church but enjoy the worship and let someone else care for the children for a while.

- Go to a weekday Bible study if possible. When my children were small, an interdenominational Bible study, called Community Bible Study, was set up in York, with a satellite group in our village. Its strongest selling point for me was not the calibre of the material or the other people joining, but the fact that it had a crèche! That Bible study was a lifeline to me at a period when my lifestyle was such that quality time alone with God was virtually impossible.

Dealing with the guilt of parenthood

This is an important issue to address when considering Jesus as Lord of our individual lives. It has been said that 'parenthood is one long guilt trip'. Even if rationally we know that we need not be guilty, we are plagued by feelings of guilt from soon after the baby's birth until . . . well, according to grandparents I have spoken to, those feelings never leave! Guilt at making them an only child or part of a huge family. Guilt at having them too close together or too far apart. Guilt about what we might have done wrong. Guilt about when we lost concentration or turned our backs and they fell down the stairs or choked on a Lego piece or pulled hot tea over themselves. Guilt about losing our tempers, shouting or smacking in anger, saying things we didn't mean. Guilt about not spending enough time with them, not stimulating them enough, not listening to them read enough or helping them with their homework. Guilt about spending too much time, so that they can't amuse or think for themselves. Guilt about going back to paid work, or having lots of people round in the evenings or going out to meetings or not watching them play football. Guilt at not liking them sometimes. The list is endless.

The participants in my parenting survey had much to say on this individual subject. The overwhelming conclusion to be drawn from their remarks is that guilt is indeed a major issue in parenting. As Christians, we can even have the extra guilt of feeling guilty! ('Well, you know, Sister, that there is now no condemnation . . . you really shouldn't feel like that.') I know that I shouldn't feel like that, but telling me so doesn't really help. What I need is some way to prevent me feeling like it in the first place. The following process has proved helpful for many:

- Try and identify the true cause of your guilty feelings. Often we articulate guilt about incidents or circumstances which are not the actual source of our feelings. You might express guilt about producing yet another convenience meal for the family instead of the freshly cooked delight you feel you should be producing. The root of your feelings, however, is that you are not sure that you are using your time aright, and perhaps you should not have taken that part-time job after all, if the family are going to suffer. The convenience meal is a symptom of those feelings, rather than their cause. Once you can pinpoint the root of your guilt, it is much easier to deal with.

- Ascertain whether the cause is really down to you or not.

Sheila Bridge, in *The Art of Plate Spinning*, differentiates between false guilt, induced by ourselves or the expectations of those around us, and true guilt. Analyse your feelings and identify whether you are actually, as she puts it, 'taking responsibility for factors that are beyond your control'. If that is the case, then the guilt is false and can be abandoned without further delay. So often we torture ourselves with reproaches for things for which we are not actually accountable at all.

- Do not allow yourself to feel guilty about things which are not your   responsibility, and don't allow others to put that guilt on you (easier said than done!). Because parenting is such a vulnerable occupation, it is very easy to be over-sensitive to the opinions of others. As one of my corres-pondents expressed it: 'When teachers and other adults criticise the children, I take it personally as a reflection of my parenting.' Don't accept that everything which goes wrong is necessarily your fault!

- If you really have done something wrong, however small, ask God's forgiveness, and anyone else's if necessary. Jesus died on the cross so that forgiveness of sins was freely and constantly available to us. Once the wrongdoing has been acknowledged and turned away from, God forgives and releases you from it.

- Believe in the forgiveness of God and your ability to make a fresh start. *'Therefore, there is now no condemnation for those who are in Christ Jesus, because through Christ Jesus the law of the Spirit of life set me free from the law of sin and death'* (Romans 8:1–2). Condemnation is life-sapping, joy-destroying and imprisoning. How wonderful that we do not have to endure it, from the Lord, other people or ourselves!

- Believe that you *are* the best person to parent your children, and that God is helping you to do the finest job possible. This is not just the power of positive thinking, it is the truth! Allow the truth to set you free (John 8:32).

- Pray, read, talk through your strategies and decisions concerning your family and then be at peace about them.

Guilt, however understandable, does not need to have a place in the life of the redeemed Christian, who has a Saviour who has taken away the root of guilt once and for all. So deal with it quickly when it does arise and be free to enjoy the Lord and all he has given you – including your children!

Maintaining a God-centred focus in our individual lives is not always easy, even when it is what we really desire. As with many other aspects of life when children are on the scene, it will not come as naturally or as spontaneously as it once did. This is not a failure on our part, it is just a fact of which we need to be aware, so that we can take the necessary measures to uphold that vital, life-giving relationship. As we get to know the Lord more, communicating with him through good times and bad, receiving and overflowing with his love and serving him in whichever ways he directs, then inevitably he will become increasingly Lord in our family as well.

Lord in our marriage

I have heard it said (though I regret to say I cannot remember by whom) that 'the best thing we can do for our children is to have a happy, stable marriage'. This is simultaneously an encouraging and a challenging thought. The ideal environment in which to bring up a family does not depend on material comforts or size of house but on the relationship of the parents. As Christians, we would believe that the happiest and most enduring marriages are those which have the Lord at their centre.

Of course, there are many people who do a wonderful job without a partner, for one reason or another, or whose partner is not a Christian, and I do not want to denigrate those people at all. No matter what our circumstances, we hang on to God's promise that he will work all things together for the best (Romans 8:28), and he has a special care for widows (and lone parents) and orphans. But the fact remains that his master plan, and therefore the best for his people, is for man and woman to be together in covenant relationship, and to bring up a family within that framework. Right at the beginning of creation, God had the blueprint for society already perfected in his mind: '*So God created man in his own image, in the image of God he created him, male and female he created them. God blessed them and said to them, "Be fruitful and increase in number; fill the earth and subdue it"* ' (Genesis 1:27–8). Of course, we can draw a spiritual application to this commission, but it is undoubtedly to be interpreted at a literal level as well.

God created man and woman to be together to reflect him in their lives and their joining, and gave them the gift of creating life within them and forming a steadfast grouping to worship and glorify him. That blueprint has not changed, despite the battering which marriage and the family have suffered down the centuries. Throughout the Bible we see instances of God's anger when the marriage covenant is broken. He enshrines the concept of monogamy and sexual purity in the Ten Commandments and refers to the sin of sexual immorality consistently in both the Old and the New Testaments. This is summed up well by the writer to the Hebrews: '*Marriage should be honoured by all, and the marriage bed kept pure, for God will judge the adulterer and all the sexually immoral*' (Hebrews 13:4).

Quite recently, a report by leading bishops in the Church of England questioned the validity of calling pre-marital sex a sin any more. John Oliver, Bishop of Hereford, was quoted as saying that the Church needed to move with the times and 'recognise the realities of social change' (*Sunday Times*, 12 October 1997). The report went on to make the point that marriage was really a Victorian idea anyway, and that in the Middle Ages people lived together ahead of the marriage ceremony. It was felt to be 'unhelpful' for the Church to maintain a strict line on sexual activity outside marriage, and many bishops said that they would be prepared to bless a cohabiting relationship. It is true that the Church needs to be in touch with the culture, and reach out in love to those who do not know Jesus. However, we cannot do that at the expense of clear biblical teaching. To ignore or contradict the Bible, God's word, in order to curry favour and look a bit more modern is a perilous path indeed. It is not fashionable to keep to biblical rules on sexual purity and family life, but it is the only way which brings true peace and security, because it is God's way. If we follow the spiritual principles of marriage and allow the Lord to be at the centre of our relationship, then we have created a solid foundation for our family life, and our parenting will prosper.

Covenant not contract

The marriage relationship is a picture of God's relationship with his people. Throughout the Bible, there are instances of him making binding covenants with his people, to express his love and commitment to them. Covenant is sometimes confused with contract, but they differ in several significant ways. Both are legal terms for a joining upheld by the law, but whereas a contract is an agreement in which both parties' main interest is to maximise what they can get out of it, a covenant has as its sole objective the passing on of some benefit. The aim of any contract negotiation is to get the best deal for yourself, but a covenant does not provide for anything in return. Many contracts contain an 'opt-out clause' which provides for the termination of the contract. It lays down how the contract may be cancelled and under what circumstances. A covenant does not. Many covenants, including the marriage covenant, are for an unlimited duration, and are therefore binding for life.

It is on covenant that marriage is built: *'the LORD is acting as the witness between you and the wife of your youth . . . your partner, the wife of your marriage covenant. Has not the LORD made them one? In flesh and spirit they are his. And why one? Because he was seeking godly offspring. So guard yourself in your spirit, and do not break faith with the wife of your youth'* (Malachi 2:14–15). Some people might be fearful of such irrevocability, but actually it is very liberating. It means that our relationship is established on something more solid and lasting than our capricious emotions. We come into the relationship in an attitude of giving rather than getting, and within the context of God's greater covenant with us. It is not that our emotions for each other will disappear, leaving us trapped in a legalistic, loveless nightmare, but that we have something more substantial than feelings on which to base our life together.

Love is not a feeling; it's a decision of the will. There are inevitably times in marriage when we do not feel 'in love' with our partner, when, frankly, we do not even like him or her very much. There are spells of tension or barrenness in any relationship, but that does not stop us loving, because love is a choice, independent of surface feelings. Our covenant with each other and with God means that we do not give up on the relationship in periods of difficulty. It means that we do not dwell on the attractive and friendly nature of the work or sport colleague, but instead rediscover the attractiveness of our marriage partner. It is not wrong to have feelings about the marriage or our partner which are sometimes negative. It is how we handle those feelings which is so crucial. Our covenant means that we do all in our power to change negative into positive, and work for the best of our partner at all times.

Captivated by love (Proverbs 5:18)

This covenant love, which God gives us, is the unconditional, totally accepting love described so beautifully in 1 Corinthians 13:

> *Love is patient, love is kind. It does not envy, it does not boast, it is not proud. It is not rude, it is not self-seeking, it is not easily angered, it keeps no record of wrongs. Love does not delight in evil, but rejoices with the truth. It always protects, always trusts, always hopes, always perseveres. Love never fails.* (1 Corinthians 13:4–8)

Run that list past your own attitudes and you may not be entirely satisfied! Yet this is the love we are to have for our spouse and then for our children. It is God-given, and therefore God-powered. He will supply our need in this area. Marital love is not some ethereal, sentimental concept; it is practical and tough as well as romantic and passionate, enduring the crises of life as well as enjoying the delights. To keep it strong and effective requires willpower and effort on our part, but it is always worthwhile. Combating the demands, stresses and sometimes sheer mundanity of daily life and preventing our love becoming stale and lifeless is a continuous process, but one that can be extremely pleasurable!

- **Make time for each other**. Most of us have hectic lifestyles, combining family, work, church and social activities, and in the effort to achieve all our goals there are inevitably some casualties. Sadly, it is often quality time with one's partner which suffers most. In the busyness of life, we see each other, but we don't actually spend much time together alone, enjoying ourselves. It can almost feel a bit of a crime to sit down together and 'do nothing' all evening except talk and sip wine! We are always so aware of all those jobs lying in wait for us. Remember all those things you used to do when you were 'going out'? Walks, visits to the cinema, meals with friends, drinks in the pub, dances, concerts, games of squash . . . Resurrect some of them! Find babysitters and make time for each other a priority.

- **Make time for God together**. Again, it is easy to crowd this important feature of marriage out of its rightful prominence in our lives. Just as married couples can become 'distant' if they do not spend sufficient time together, so can our relationship with the Lord suffer. We might manage to pray or read the Bible alone, but rarely come together to worship, pray or study the word. Like so many other aspects of marriage and parenting, it is difficult to do, but invaluable and highly enjoyable once you have made the effort! If necessary, schedule some time into your diaries to pray and worship as a couple. This seems rather artificial, but you do it with other friends, so why not with your greatest friend? Then if someone rings and asks to come round on a certain night, or there is a social at school, you can say that you already have a meeting scheduled for that evening. It really should take precedence over everything else. Be natural together in the presence of God, expressing yourselves to him without self-consciousness. You will discover new depths in your relationship with the Lord and with each other, and new resources for the tasks he has given you to do.

- **Keep the romance going!** This is more difficult when surrounded by noisy, demanding, sometimes dirty, smelly children! Somehow, the ambience doesn't seem quite right! However, romance is more dependent on an attitude than external circumstances. Do you still view your husband as a dashing, handsome beau, who makes your heart race and your knees go weak? Is your wife still that enigmatic beauty whose personality and physique seemed to invade all your senses? Or have you begun to take each other for granted? Can romance survive the early morning bleariness of endless disturbed nights? (Disturbed by children, that is, not by passion!) The answer is yes, with a little imagination!

There are many ways to maintain romantic touches in your life, but the basis of them is your determination to remain 'in love' with your spouse. Determination sounds a bit unromantic, I know, but that is often what it takes! The traditional flowers and chocolates are always welcome, but other small gestures can transform your perspective on each other. A candle on the meal table, a note hidden in a drawer or in the packed lunch, a suggestive phone call, a surprise evening out, taking special care with your appearance, a small gift . . . be creative, but most of all, continue, whenever possible, to consider your partner in a romantic light. Obviously, that cannot happen all the time; changing nappies, emptying the bin and sorting out disputes are never going to be romantic activities, but the underlying assumption of romance can remain unscathed

It is important to treat each other with courtesy and consideration, as you did in the early days. It's a sad reflection that often married couples are far more polite to strangers than they ever are to each other. Common civility will make all the difference to your mutual perceptions.

We have been married nearly fifteen years now, and we are still very romantic in our approach to each other, despite the demands of a busy life and the undisputed mundanity of many household routines. Graham travels abroad a fair amount with his job, and whenever he is due back, I feel as excited as if we were going out on a date in our early days of courting!

- **Be demonstrative**. This is closely akin to being romantic, in that a demonstration of your feelings for each other is extremely valuable in maintaining romance. However, being demonstrative extends to others besides yourselves. Your marriage is a joint venture in the community, and together you can have an impact on those around you. It is important that you express your love to each other and then to those with whom you have contact. Love cannot be taken for granted ('You know I love you. I don't have to keep saying so!'); it should be demonstrated to the world! This can be through verbal and physical expression, through hospitality and practical care. Be free with touch and hugs, to each other, your children and to those you know. Our children always pretend to be cameramen when we kiss in their presence, and crowd round for close-ups, with accompanying sound-tracks (such as 'Yuk!'). But they like us showing affection in this way, and sometimes order us to kiss, particularly if we have just had a difference of opinion about something!

Sometimes, even comparative strangers can benefit from a physical declaration of our care for them, if they are in pain of any sort. I was talking to someone the other day who had recently lost her husband. As we talked, her eyes filled, and though I did not know her very well I instinctively put my arms round her and gave her a hug, because that was what she needed. Express appreciation and love for one another in spoken and written words. Send cards to those that you know are having a hard time, make meals for those who are ill or at a crisis point in their lives. British people generally are very reticent about being demonstrative, but as Christians we can point the way to a more expressive society! When God is Lord in our marriage, we as a couple will be an illustration of love in all its facets to those around us.

• **Don't leave sex to the last minute!** Well, of course, we all do sometimes; in fact there are times when we leave it so late that it doesn't happen at all! However, if this becomes the norm rather than the exception, then it is time to reconsider priorities and get down to some deep communicating on the subject. If you are making time for each other and for God, being romantic some of the time and demonstrating your love for each other, then sex should be a large part of your life together. If it isn't, then don't feel a failure! But do consider some of the aspects of your life to see whether there is an imbalance which is causing this lack. I am saddened at the number of people I know for whom the act of making love is not much more than a chore, performed at the end of a day full of chores, when tiredness is the overwhelming sensation. All of my conversations on the subject (not that I talk about it all the time!) have been with women, so I would not like to comment on whether there are many men who feel the same, but on the whole I would guess not. Men seem much more able to switch into and out of sex, perhaps because they are more strongly driven by their physical feelings. A woman, on the other hand, generally needs to be 'in the mood' before she is ready to enter fully into lovemaking. Often, through lack of time or energy, or because of tensions in the relationship, she will make love out of a sense of duty rather than because she really wants to. This can breed resentment and unfulfilment, and so a vicious circle begins which sometimes spirals into problems and even breakdown.

Sexual intercourse is one of the Lord's most precious and exciting gifts to us – for procreation, yes, but also, emphatically, for our pleasure as well. One only has to glance in the Bible to know that. When God first institutes marriage, in Genesis, he makes mention of the physical union of man and woman as a key part in his purposes: '*For this reason, a man will leave his father and mother and be united to his wife, and they will become one flesh*' (Genesis 2:24). Becoming 'one flesh' sexually is a symbol of God's union with his people and a sealing of the covenant between them. It is a vital part of marriage, not just because it produces children and stops us from 'burning' (1 Corinthians 7:9), but because it deepens our understanding of the 'holy mystery' that is Christ's union with the Church. There are many images of marriage in the Bible, and many use the metaphor of sexual union to depict the Lord's relationship with his people.

So sex is a spiritual activity, an act of worship, to be enjoyed to the full, as worship should be. It is an ongoing declaration of commitment, a bestowing of self on each other, a surrendering of will to one another, a mutual over-flowing of joy and pleasure.

Such a gift should not be misused or neglected. Set aside time for it, using opportunities at any time of the day, rather than always waiting until the night, when you are both tired. Admittedly, this is easier said than done, particularly with young children, but with ingenuity it can be done! Leave the chores until later and leap (or fall!) into bed as soon as the children are asleep. Take half a day's holiday and spend it in bed. ('When have *we* ever done that?' asks Graham indignantly. Well, it's good to have ideals to aim for, isn't it?) Increase anticipation verbally and physically during the day. Be creative in the way you approach lovemaking (variety is the spice . . . !). Without being obsessive, make sex a focus in your life!

Communication is the key

Picture another scene. Yet again, you have been left to clear up the mess in the kitchen while your partner has gone to 'get on' with some important project (like studying the sport in the newspaper, you grimly speculate). His claims to be a New Man ring hollow in this blatant undervaluing and unappreciating of yourself. He comes in (perhaps attracted by the loud bangs and crashes as you put things away), and enquires if you are OK.

'Absolutely fine,' you reply, through gritted teeth.

'Oh good,' he says as he disappears again, 'I thought for a moment that you were upset about something.'

An implausible cameo, perhaps, but maybe not so very far removed from our own experience. Such incidents, and others similar (and I'm sure we can all think of one) might seem trivial, yet they can build up into enormous obstacles if not dealt with. So often, we fail to communicate properly with those we love best, and gradually this failure grows into a total breakdown. Statistics have shown that the most common root cause for the increasing number of divorces today is a lack of true communication, and therefore an inability to handle the conflicts and tensions which inevitably arise in human relationships.

Living and sharing with the person you love is a deeply enriching experience, bringing happiness and security, but it has its down-side as well. Those very differences which attracted in the first place can be supremely irritating in the context of everyday life. Misunderstandings and moods grow into underlying resentments, and suddenly that feeling of overwhelming love no longer seems to exist. The communication barrier has been erected, and only careful work will dismantle it before it becomes insurmountable.

One of the main reasons for this is that we do not always say what we really mean. We expect our partner to understand the subtext of our message, and we get upset if he or she fails to do so. Listening to the underlying message, reading body language, feeding back what you think you have heard and giving your partner space to express him- or herself fully before jumping in with your next thought are all important communication skills which need constant practice and refinement.

Coping with conflict

As has been said before, conflict is inevitable between people living closely together. However great your love for each other, you are not going to agree on everything all the time. Life brings its stresses and strains, and these will intensify any areas of discord already existing and perhaps create a few more. Yet this need not be a negative aspect in your relationship. Conflict, if handled correctly, can be a growth point rather than a breakpoint.

One of the most difficult elements of managing conflict is learning how to handle anger in a positive manner. So many people think that anger is a sinful emotion, but it is not; like any other feeling, it is neutral. It is what we do with it that can become unrighteous. Jesus was angry at times during his earthly ministry, and he was without sin. To feel angry is like a smoke alarm, alerting us to danger ahead. If we ignore it, there will be a damaging blaze. The anger itself is a warning signal. Venting anger uncontrollably can do great damage; hurtful words are said that can take a long time to heal, and the very force of the emotion can be frightening and destroy some of the love between us. Yet suppressing or ignoring angry feelings is also harmful, as they will turn inwards and breed resentment and depression.

If you are in a conflict situation, attempt to control your speech until your emotion has calmed down a little. Examine why you feel as you do, and try to talk through those feelings. What was it about the incident that made you so angry? Usually, the event itself was merely a trigger for underlying feelings which have not been properly dealt with before. If you, like me, are of a volatile temperament, then you might need to withdraw for a little while before you can be sufficiently in control to analyse and express your reactions. In those circumstances, I will say: 'I feel very angry about this, but I don't want to talk about it at the moment.' Then, if possible, I will spend some time alone, allowing myself to cool down and discover what the real problem is, before talking it over with Graham and making things right again.

When there is repentance, forgiveness and understanding on

both sides, then inevitably the bond between you improves. Of course, it doesn't always work like that, and I lose my temper and shout, which just makes everything worse and puts me in the wrong when I may not necessarily have been so originally! However, failure to follow the correct principles does not negate those principles, and so we should always aim to cope with conflict by talking through our feelings about its causes, and seeking and offering forgiveness for any wrongdoing involved. We usually find that we have got to know each other so much better through such painful times, and that they are a springboard to a new stage in our relationship.

God wants to be Lord in our lives and Lord in our marriage and, being the loving Dad he is, he gives us help to enable him to be so. He does not impose himself as Lord. It is our choice, but by his Holy Spirit he gives us the power to submit ourselves to him, and the practical help to allow it to happen. All he requires is the desire in us to have him as Lord, and he will do the rest. And because of his great love for us, he does not condemn and dispossess us when we fail to defer to his lordship, but gently encourages us back in the right way again.

5

Relationship, not Religion

Let the little children come to me and do not hinder them, for the
kingdom of heaven belongs to such as these.
(Matthew 19:14)

Lord in our child's life

Commitment or copying?

Every Christian parent's ultimate desire for their children is
that they will have a living, vital, enduring faith of their own.
The scary bit is that it is our responsibility to nurture and
encourage that faith. Of course, only the Lord can create his
new life in a person, and each individual is accountable to him
for their own response finally, but the Lord gives to parents the
task of teaching their children about him: '*These commandments
that I give you today are to be upon your hearts. Impress them on
your children. Talk about them when you sit at home and when you
walk along the road, when you lie down and when you get up*'
(Deuteronomy 6:6–7). Our most important goal must be to
introduce our children to Jesus as a person, to God as a father,
and to the Holy Spirit as a helper, rather than imposing a set of
religious 'do's and don'ts' on young people.

Many parents are unsure if and when a child is ready to make
a true commitment to the Lord, and it is a complex question.

Children always want to please their parents (well, young ones do at any rate!) and so will emulate their lifestyle and beliefs, without completely comprehending for themselves. It is just something they have grown up with and take for granted. Sensitive parents are concerned about brainwashing and about how to translate this imitation into reality in the child's life. There is nothing essentially wrong with imitation initially. (Paul, for instance, urges his readers to imitate him, as a father in the faith, in 1 Corinthians 4:16), and we must ensure, as previously discussed, that what they copy is a true faith and not a sham. Children learn everything by copying, and spiritual beliefs will not be an exception. The Bible says that your family will be sanctified by your faith, until such time as they can make their own decisions (1 Corinthians 7:14). In my many years in children's ministry, I have seen children as young as five or six years old who had a very real relationship with God, and at the other end of the spectrum I have seen others who had all the 'right' answers off pat (whoever she is) but who evidently did not enjoy a living relationship with the Lord.

It is our task to tell our children about Jesus, explaining simply the basic message of salvation and eternal life, to help the Bible come to life for them and to lead them into worship. The reality of Christianity is something they will absorb through their daily lives, and there will probably be a significant point when they are a little older, perhaps at a meeting or camp, when they reaffirm their beliefs, and their relationship with the Lord will enter a new dimension.

All of our children would say they were Christians. They cannot remember a particular time when they first knew and accepted Jesus. They have always known him and talked to him and about him as part of their everyday lives. They enjoy meeting with the rest of the church on Sundays. Sometimes they just sit on their seats and appear to be quite detached from all that is going on. At other times they worship God unself-consciously and even contribute prayers or 'pictures'. When they don't feel like worshipping, they don't do it. Hopefully, one day they will learn that it is important to praise and honour the King no matter how they feel, but for the moment it is enough that they are part of what is going on. We talk about the meeting afterwards, and their own meetings, but we never tell them what they should do during the worship, because that must come from their own heart of love for the Lord, not out of a sense of wanting to please us. They know Jesus, and they are well taught in the principles of the faith, but inevitably there will come a time when their beliefs are tested and they will have to decide for themselves the reality of what they have known.

This often happens during the teen years, when the urge to question all the values and philosophies with which you have been brought up is most strong. There are many Christian parents at present, faithful people who have followed the Lord for many years, who are struggling with the pain of children who have gone away from God. Inevitably, they blame themselves, which can often increase the tension in the household. The teenager senses the disappointment, concern and disapproval, even if it is not articulated directly. This makes him take a more obstinate position than he actually feels, and so the problem continues.

Often, the teen who has decided to abandon the values of his childhood goes to a further opposite extreme than his peer who has been brought up in comparative apathy. Not all teenagers dye their hair purple and wear a nose ring, but the son of some good friends of ours, who was a Christian until fairly recently, has done just that! The most important course of action in these situations is to continue affirming the child and expressing unconditional love towards him. The teenager is confused inside, unsure of his identity, needing boundaries as much as ever but wanting to set his own, wanting to be free of authority while still desiring its security. If the parents can remain calm, loving and communicating through this phase, then long term damage will be avoided. Like many other aspects of parenting, it is not easy, but the Lord is able to give us the power to achieve it.

The teen years are not the only ones, though, where our children may choose to turn their backs on all that they have known. We know someone who was a model teenager. The son of a minister, he remained in the Christian youth scene and appeared to be maintaining a close relationship with the Lord. He did not rebel against his parents, and they had great expectations of him doing important exploits for God. He married a Christian girl – not someone his parents felt completely comfortable about, but at least she was a Christian. They had three children and then, gradually, flaws which perhaps had always been underlying in his life became perceptible. He and his wife drifted away from the Church, away from the Lord. He started spending a lot of time with a work colleague and eventually left his wife and family to live with her. It was a complete rejection of all that he had been taught and apparently lived for for so long. When the test came, his own relationship with God was not strong enough to withstand it.

We must be very careful as parents that we do not allow our children to be too reliant on our own faith, but instead encourage them to become independent in their thinking, study and experience of the Lord. 'Yes, but how?' you may justifiably be thinking. I don't think that there are any simple answers. Certainly, if you are living life to the full with the Lord yourselves, there is far more likelihood that your children will experience his reality for themselves. However, even that is not necessarily enough to prevent them thinking that you are nutters at some point in their lives! It is important not to pressure them with your own hopes and fears for them in the spiritual sphere. Talk to them about their beliefs and your own faith. Be natural in your conversation about the Lord, as if you were talking about a friend, but don't embarrass them by 'preaching' at any of their non-Christian visitors! Keep hold of

God's promise that his word will never be planted in vain:

> *As the rain and the snow come down from heaven,*
> *and do not return to it without watering the earth,*
> *and making it bud and flourish,*
> *so that it yields seed for the sower and bread for the eater,*
> *so is my word that goes out from my mouth:*
> *it will not return to me empty,*
> *but will accomplish what I desire and*
> *achieve the purpose for which I sent it.*
> *You will go out in joy and be led forth in peace.* (Isaiah 55:10–12)

God is faithful, and when you have done all that you can, then rest in the knowledge that he will keep his promises. Nothing can separate us from God's love, once we have chosen to accept it.

The pull of peer pressure

Being different in a secular society is not easy for anyone, and particularly not for a child or emerging adult. In the early days, it is the parent who decides what is acceptable out of the world's culture and what is not, and different parents have varying degrees of strictness about this. For instance, we have never allowed the boys to have toy guns or other weapons. We have explained that as killing is evil and not what God likes, then we would prefer them not to make it into a game. Violence is becoming so normal in this society that everyone is growing immune to it. Other Christian parents, however, feel that this is extreme and that there is no harm in allowing children to play soldiers or other games involving weapons.

We do not make a huge issue about it, for we are no more right than the person with the opposite view. We just have to act as our feelings dictate on such matters and hope that our children understand. It does not seem to have been a problem to them, and there has been no secret compensatory aggression arising from the ban. We make sure that they have plenty of other exciting activities, and we also encourage them occasionally to think about the victims of violence and the consequences of war. That sounds dreadfully 'heavy', but is not so (honestly!) within the context of helping them to develop empathy for those around them. All parents have their own opinions about what is or is not good for their children from the prevailing culture, and it is for them to make decisions after praying about them. Sometimes they might be open to negotiation as time passes (our children won the right to water pistols in the summer), and sometimes the principles are unchanging.

As the child grows older and more mature, he will have to choose for himself how much he gets involved in his peer culture or, perhaps more tellingly, how much he can withstand the very real pressure involved in that culture. Children are made to feel inadequate or 'uncool' if they don't wear the right designer labels or listen to the right music. 'But everyone in my class . . .' becomes a familiar refrain as your children try to persuade you to buy an outrageously expensive garment or let them watch an unsuitable video.

It is worth deciding beforehand how much you are prepared to force them to be different, and how much you are going to allow them to conform. Keep an ear open to the prevailing youth trends and decide where you stand on them before they become an issue. Is Polly Pocket worth the tears and frustration of denial? Is it OK for your children to abandon all their smart clothes in favour of a nylon tracksuit with stripes down the side? What is a tamagotchi anyway? Sometimes, financial restrictions mean that it is not possible to give in to the latest trend, even if you wanted to, but do not use the 'we can't afford it' option as a way of avoiding debate as to why you do not agree with the trend in question. We have had some valuable family discussions about the power of advertising, the dangers of being unduly influenced by peer pressure, the inadvisability of too much 'junk' music, television or video games.

We would always forbid extremes – what we would consider actively against the word of God, such as some of the more violent videos and computer games – and, as previously mentioned, we are fairly strict about their television consumption, even if all their friends do watch certain programmes. But in other areas we allow them to join in with the current craze if only in moderate form: making our own Tracey Island when Thunderbirds were all the rage, instead of buying one; buying a pop CD for our teenager for Christmas, but making sure that there is some good Christian music around as well; allowing them to have small merchandising from their favourite football clubs, but not buying the full strips . . . and so the list goes on!

Fear of being laughed at or teased is a very strong force in most children, and these days Christianity is held up as a figure of fun and scorn. To admit to a faith is to invite jeering and even bullying. We encourage our children always to stand up for what is right, for instance taking an unpopular person's side if they are being 'picked on' or hurt, and not to go with the crowd when they know the crowd is doing wrong. If they are too susceptible to the power of the gang, then they are in danger of getting involved in all sorts of activities that will do them enormous damage. Most youngsters start smoking and drugs and even sex as a result of duress from their friends. They do not want to seem a wimp or 'scared'. They want to identify with the group, because they are in the process of defining their own identities, and because they hate the humiliation of being laughed at. They cannot see beyond the emotion of the moment, and it is hard for parents, or even the Lord, to compete with that.

We can only assure them of our love and keep the channels of communication open. If, in a quiet, companionable moment, we can talk to them about the hazards of peer pressure, without denigrating their friends, and about the joy of keeping to God's ways, then we are making good progress through the minefields of adolescence.

Of course, for that companionable moment to arise, we have to be around for our children. Lots of parents said to us when the children were younger, 'Once they get to the teens, you never see them. They're either off out with their friends, or they're in their rooms, listening to pop music or playing on the computer.' However, that has not really been our experience, nor do we want it to be so. In some ways, the children need us more now that they are older than when they were younger. Whereas we used to be able to go out in the evening, leaving the babysitter with all five asleep by eight o'clock, with several hours ahead of us, now most of the evening is taken up chatting to them, helping with topics, listening to reading, pottering around so that we're there if they need us. Some of our most significant conversations with them have been as we have been putting them to bed. Rob Parsons, in his book *The Sixty Minute Father* (Hodder and Stoughton, 1995), points out that 'quality time' with children usually comes out of hours of 'unquality' time, when you are just there, doing chores, sitting in the same room together, engaged on a joint project, chatting about inconsequentialities. Because your relationship has been built up through the ordinariness as well as the fun of family life, then your children will find it natural and desirable to share with you their deeper feelings and listen to what you have to say on the more serious matters of life.

Graham and I have never put pressure on our children to talk about their Christianity to their friends, reasoning that their views and behaviour should speak for themselves and that we should be sensitive to the very real agonies that children can suffer at the hands of their peers. Our prayer is that gradually their faith will give them a confidence and self-esteem which will enable them to be receptive to the Holy Spirit and to talk about the Lord when he prompts them to.

Lord in our family life

God confers a great deal of importance on the family unit. Throughout the Bible, there are references to the family and its significance in God's purposes. The Church is frequently referred to as a family (Galatians 6:10) with God as the heavenly Father and Jesus as brother and co-heir (Hebrews 2:11). The family is God's means of demonstrating his love and his ways, and is one of his methods of reaching those who don't know him. In Isaiah, he makes this very clear: *'Here am I, and the children the* LORD *has given me. We are signs and symbols in Israel from the* LORD *Almighty, who dwells on Mount Zion'* (Isaiah 8:18). Signs and symbols are means of indicating and interpreting the truth. A sign points the way for those who do not know it, and proclaims facts for those passing by. A symbol helps to explain complicated concepts in a simplified manner, so that all can understand. What a privilege that God has chosen us to do such an important job!

For our own and other people's sakes, therefore, it is vital that our family expresses the life and principles of our Lord. The problem is that there are inevitably many times when our family does not express this life, and this can lead to additional stress as we feel that we have let the Lord down and that we are not becoming the sort of family he desires. Dr James Dobson, the Christian childcare expert, tells a wonderful story about how he once gave a talk on disciplining children with both his children, then aged five and nine, present. Afterwards, as he was 'dispensing profound child-rearing wisdom like a vending machine' to a crowd of eager parents, he heard a terrible crash on the balcony of the church building, followed by thundering feet and childish shrieks of laughter. He looked up to see his children racing around causing havoc. As he said, 'It was one of the most embarrassing moments of my life. I could hardly go on telling the lady in front of me how to manage her children when mine were going crazy on the balcony.' (James Dobson, *The New Dare to Discipline*, Kingsway Publications Ltd, 1993).

Such incidents are all too common in the Christian family's experience. I remember when we first met Graham's new boss as a family. He came to the campsite near his home in Germany, where we had arrived late, tired and rather harassed. When we had pitched camp, he suggested going out to a local restaurant for a meal, to which he generously proposed to treat us. The children had already been rather difficult as we had been putting up the tents, racing around noisily and responding to our requests for help with 'Do I have to?' (Perhaps it was too dark for them to notice our 'non-verbal' communication!) At the restaurant, to our horror, they began to object to the food provided (unusual for them!) and to squabble over who had what. I was mortified, and could only hope that either his English was not up to the nuances of children's disputes, or that Graham would hold him in sparkling conversation for the whole evening while I tried to keep the children in order. We certainly were not a good advertisement for family life that night! Most people probably have similar tales to tell, or whole phases of their lives when they do not feel as if God is Lord in their family.

What we have to remember is that the issue is not whether we have a perfect family life but how we handle the failures and the difficult patches. For there will be difficult patches, because the home is the environment within which the child matures and learns, physically, mentally, socially, emotionally and spiritually, secure in the love which allows him to make mistakes and get it wrong. It is in the family that he discovers how to relate to others, to take turns, to care for people, to submit to authority, to express anger appropriately, to accept criticism and to distinguish right from wrong. This is no easy process, and as adults we know that we have not achieved it all, so it is inevitable that there will be times when attitudes are not right, when behaviour is atrocious, when irresponsibility predominates, and when chaos reigns (and that's just among the parents!).

Allowing God to be Lord in our family life is not a case of having perfectly behaved children, but of acknowledging him as being in control (even when it doesn't seem like it) and maintaining a vital relationship with him throughout all the pressures and challenges. The principles he gives for family life are there for our blessing, not as a banner of failure; he does not expect us to succeed in all of them immediately, but with his help they can be a firm foundation, undergirding our attitudes and actions.

Some principles for family life

'He who fears the LORD has a secure fortress, and for his children it will be a refuge' (Proverbs 14:26).

Talk about the Lord

'We will not hide them from children; we will tell the next generation the praiseworthy deeds of the LORD, his power and the wonders he has done . . . so that the next generation would know them . . . Then they would put their trust in God and would not forget his deeds but would keep his commands' (Psalm 78:4,6–7). Some admirable families have a regular prayer and worship time, and even Bible study. I read one book where the four children are ready at the table every morning before school for a time of prayer. If you can manage this, it is a marvellous way to acknowledge God as Lord in your family. It also instils spiritual discipline in the children and strengthens them for the day ahead.

However, I have to confess that we have never been able to achieve a regular family time, though we often try. We do have times when we come together to pray and we do pray with each child individually every night. The Lord is included in our conversation frequently. We talk about what he has done in individual lives and what he has done in the church. We discuss what he might think about various topics of news, either local or wider, and what he says in his word. We point out that he does not enjoy bad behaviour, and require that people ask his forgiveness as well as that of the person they have wronged. Family worship and Bible study are frankly more ad hoc than we would like, and we are working on it! It is good for the children to pray and worship together, and we encourage them to hear from the Lord themselves. It is perfectly possible for God to speak through a child, either directly or through a Bible verse or 'picture'. Expect such events in your family, and respond when they happen!

Unconditional love

This is becoming a recurring theme, but I do not apologise for any repetition of the subject, because it is of such vital importance in bringing up children. If God is Lord in our family life, then he must be reflected in the unreserved love that we lavish on our children. Tell them frequently that they are loved, no matter what they do or fail to do. They are loved for who they are. Make it clear that you enjoy their company and praise them enthusi–astically for their good attitudes and actions. Children so desperately need the security of knowing God's love, and the first way they will experience it is through the family.

Teach and encourage your children to extend that uncon-ditional love to each other. This is quite difficult, because children seem to be born with an innate streak of competitive-ness towards their siblings. My friends' younger son's long-held ambition, for example, was to be older than his brother Michael. When he reached an age to understand that this would never happen, he was devastated!

Like the vast majority of parents, we have always tried to treat each of our children equally, and have deliberately not encouraged a competitive spirit in the family. Yet despite all our strictures that no one is better than anyone else, that we love them all the same, that when the younger ones are older they will have the same privileges currently enjoyed by the older ones, that it doesn't really matter if someone has a few more crisps on their plate, our boys still seem to be obsessed with fairness to the point of unkindness. It is frustrating and demoralising, because we cannot seem to make them realise that their disagreeable squabbles over whose turn it is to sit in the front, or what time others go to bed, are trivial.

Their knowledge that we love them absolutely is not sufficient to prevent them clinging on to the perceived expressions of their importance in the family. It's as if they have a status to maintain which is manifested in the privileges and responsibilities each assumes for himself. Yet we have never sanctioned such a way of thinking. We can only continue to affirm our love for them, correct any wrong attitudes and perceptions and show them how to express love to each other. It is as important that they are as secure in each other's love as they are in ours. Otherwise, they will grow apart as they grow older, a subconscious rivalry and fear of criticism and unfavourable comparison building a wall between them. Unconditional love is a bedrock of family life and an indication of God's rule within it.

Discipline

Biblical principles of discipline have been a topic of controversy for a long time. Very often the subject is narrowed to mean punishment, whereas actually it is much wider than that. The contentious issue of smacking, made even more current by various cases against parents being taken to the European Court, must be seen within the greater context of discipline as a whole.

Discipline is defined as 'instruction, training of the mind or body or moral faculties, subjection to authority, self-control'. The word is from the same root as 'disciple', meaning 'one who receives instruction from another, a follower'. Our children, when they are young, are our disciples, following our instruction and adhering to our philosophy of life. It is our responsibility to instruct well, in content and in method. Discipline is the means by which we assist our offspring towards mature, self-disciplined, fulfilled adulthood. It is a training tool, not a weapon of punishment, and it originates from love for the child, not out of anger or negative feelings. From the earliest days, when we encourage the baby to reach out for toys and sit up unaided, to the young adult years, when we learn to let go and allow them to take full responsibility for their own lives, the 'on-the-job' training continues.

The difficult part of discipline arises when our small 'disciples' decide that they do not want to be subject to authority or receive instruction. The clash of wills, which begins in small ways in infancy, reaches a peak around the age of two, and then persists in waves of varying intensity throughout childhood, reaching another peak during the teenage years. Don't panic and feel that your parenting has suddenly taken a steep nose-dive, for this is a necessary stage in child development. Deep in your cute, adorable little baby's character is a streak of rebellious self-centredness which will manifest itself one way or another during the growing-up process. Our task, and it is no easy one, is to demonstrate the fundamentals of right and wrong and the importance of obedience and a submissive attitude. Dr Dobson has many valuable insights on the question of discipline, and his books have been a valuable resource for a generation of parents. His analysis of the human condition as exemplified in the young child is second to none!

This century has seen huge pendulum swings in teaching on the disciplining of children, from the harsh, almost oppressive stance taken at the turn of the century, the 'children should be seen and not heard' school of thought, to the completely child-centred 'let them express all their feelings and never tell them they are wrong' teaching of the 1960s. Now, as the century draws to a close, we see the confusion resulting from such pendulum swings. People are not sure what is the best way to bring up their children. They do what comes instinctively, but feel guilty about it, or else they abscond from the responsibility altogether, leaving it to teachers and social workers. The question boils down, really, to the basics of life with children. What *do* you do when your child deliberately does the opposite of what you tell him to do? What *do* you say when your teenager treats you with utter contempt? How do you teach them right from wrong, when all that they hear and see seems to be the exact opposite?

As you might expect, God has much to say on the subject, and provides practical help for the struggling parent. First of all, although (or rather, because) he is love, (1 John 4:16), God does believe in discipline and within that, punishment. In Proverbs, he commands us: '*Discipline your son, for in that there is hope*' (Proverbs 19:18), and '*My son, do not despise the LORD's discipline and do not resent his rebuke, because the LORD disciplines those he loves, as a father the son he delights in*' (Proverbs 3:11). Therefore, discipline cannot, of itself, be wrong, as some have claimed over the years. Maybe the way we sometimes go about it may not be right, but the general principle is from the Lord. The book of Proverbs has many insights into God's view on the matter, and they are continued in the New Testament:

Endure hardship as discipline; God is treating you as sons. For what son is not disciplined by his father? If you are not disciplined (and everyone undergoes discipline), then you are illegitimate children and not true sons. Moreover, we have all had human fathers who disciplined us and we respected them for it . . . No discipline seems pleasant at the time, but painful. Later on, however, it produces a harvest of righteousness and peace for those who have been trained by it. (Hebrews 12:7–11)

It is worth labouring the point that God, in his love, is prepared to impose severity on us for our long-term peace and happiness. This is the model we need to follow in our parenting, no matter what the childcare fad of the moment happens to be. Our aim is to bring our children up in the ways of the Lord, where they will find true fulfilment and the very best life they could have. This will inevitably involve pain at times, for ourselves as well as our children, as they learn to submit (but not submerge) their wills, bending their spirits to the ultimate authority without breaking them.

All our children have very different personalities, and have responded to discipline in correspondingly distinct ways. Some have been happy to accept what they are told, and comply without too much complaint, whereas others have resisted authority from the outset, choosing, when very young, to oppose any direction (often even when it was something fun for them!). Some have instinctively fitted in with the general family flow, whereas others have stood against it at every opportunity. We have had whingers and tantrummers, yellers and moaners, dramatic displays and quiet disappearances!

As they have grown up a little, we are beginning to see the fruits of our discipline policy, in that they do have a respect for authority, they have a strongly developed sense of right and wrong, they are reasonably obedient, they don't lie, they are caring and they are happy (most of the time!). You will see from the rest of the book that they are by no means perfect and that we still have a long way to go, but the foundation has been laid and, as with everything else, it is a matter of faith. We believe that the general principles of discipline that we apply are biblically based and that, though we make frequent mistakes, God will still bless our efforts to follow his ways. Some useful pointers regarding discipline have been culled from ongoing (sometimes bitter!) experience.

- **Decide in advance what your policy is**. Talk and pray about what is acceptable and unacceptable in behaviour and speech, so that you are prepared when incidents arise. Be clear about what conduct merits what punishment. You may have differences of opinion about these issues and it is good to sort them out in peace and quiet beforehand, rather than in the heat of the moment.

- **Use positive incentives to good behaviour**. Discipline is 'carrot and stick'. Make the carrot attractive – praise, affirmation, treats, fun – and use the stick sparingly. Some people use 'star charts' to encourage good behaviour, where designated goals earn a star if achieved. An accumulation of stars then leads to a treat or money. There are accusations of bribery in this method, but I think it depends how it is used. We have used star charts in phases successfully, but could not keep them up for any length of time – the accounting procedure took too long!

- **Forestall and distract wherever possible**. Predict the consequences of a course of action and try to prevent the inevitable if you can! For example, keep things out of reach rather than constantly telling your toddler not to touch. Or if you know that certain instructions are going to be unpopular with your teenager and cause bad attitudes to arise, give plenty of warning and integrate some sort of incentive to them.

- **Punish defiance, not irresponsibility**. Many of a child's worst actions are not deliberate. Covering the wall in Vaseline or throwing eggs on the floor are not naughty if the young child has not been forbidden to do it, nor is making loud personal remarks about people on the bus. That is what Dobson defines as 'childish irresponsibility' and should not be punished, merely pointed out as a bad idea for future reference! If, however, a child does something far less dramatic, but as a deliberate act of defiance, then that should be punished immediately. What punishment you mete out is your decision, but it must be prompt and leave the child in no doubt that disobedience doesn't pay.

• **Ensure the child is warned about the consequences of disobedience**. This is setting boundaries. The child needs to know what he is and is not allowed to do and what will happen if he transgresses the boundaries. Be very clear and deliberate about this, otherwise you are being unfair on the child and putting yourself in the wrong.

• **Always explain your actions as you go through the process**. Discipline is a learning process, and children will learn the principles if they are explained to them as they go along. Whatever disciplinary action you are taking, make sure that you have explained the procedure plainly. (For instance, 'I told you not to throw your sister's doll out of the window, but you still did it. That was disobedient. You didn't do what Mummy said. Now your sister is upset because her doll is broken, and I'm upset because you have been disobedient. What happens when you are disobedient? Yes. So now I am going to give you a smack/ send you to your room/ stop you having a treat/ make you sit on the stair, etc. to teach you not to be disobedient.') Otherwise, the child becomes confused, knowing he has offended somehow, but not sure why he is in trouble, nor what he is supposed to do next.

- **Always follow up with repentance, forgiveness and recon-
ciliation**. *'Those whom I love I rebuke and discipline. So be
earnest, and repent'* (Revelation 3:19). We discipline our
children because we love them, and it is vital that they know
that. Whatever steps you have taken should bring about true
sorrow for the action, and a determination not to do it again.
Be generous rather than grudging with forgiveness, and
make sure that it is given with a hug or cuddle and verbal
expressions of love. Once he has forgiven, God puts our
wrongdoing out of his mind forever (Psalm 103:12). We must
do the same, and reassure the child that we have done so. In
this way, they are secure in our disciplining, and there are
no undercurrents of resentment, fear or anger left to pollute
our relationship.

These principles hold good for children of any age, though
obviously the way in which we talk to them and the type of
sanctions we employ will change as the child grows older. By
the time he is a teenager, there will be much more negotiation
and discussion in the setting of boundaries, but once they are
set, it is important that they are adhered to. It is possible to
negotiate sanctions as well, so that the teen begins to take more
responsibility for the consequences of his actions. A book
that covers this angle very well is *Parenting Teenagers* by Bob
Myers.

Any discussion on discipline is not complete without considering the issue of physical correction. Understandably, with
all the horrific stories emerging about physically and sexually
abused children, there has been a revulsion against smacking
or hitting children at all. While no one in their right minds
would condone the violence and hitting in anger which has
become so normal in some households, there is a difference
between that and judicious use of physical correction. I asked
many people what their methods of discipline were, and most
admitted to smacking 'as a last resort', 'to my shame', 'when I

lose my cool'. To apply a smack as part of a policy of discipline seems to those people to be too cold and hard; smacking can only be justified when the parent has been driven to it by the extreme behaviour of the child. However, that is actually the wrong way round.

The Bible is clear that physical punishment as part of loving discipline is permissible. The most famous verse (hated by generations of children!) is from Proverbs: '*He who spares the rod hates his son, but he who loves him is careful to discipline him*' (Proverbs 13:24). There are many other verses, though, which confirm this view that physical correction is an integral part of discipline. These words, for instance: '*Folly is bound up in the heart of a child, but the rod of discipline will drive it far from him*' (Proverbs 22:15). It is clear, therefore, that smacking is only justified when it is part of an overall strategy of loving, secure discipline.

It should not be used indiscriminately, but for specific, pre-determined 'wrongs': disobedience and rebellion. These are attitudes which strike at the root of 'original sin' – the desire to go your own way rather than God's – and they need addressing at the earliest opportunity. A smack is painful but immediate, clear-cut and effective. Young children will not connect a long-drawn-out punishment with its cause, particularly if the cause was a wrong attitude rather than a specific action. If a child yells 'No!' at you when you ask him to do something, he needs an immediate response, not something which will build resentment and affirm the very attitude you are trying to correct. I have talked to young adults who have undergone this type of discipline in their childhood, and without exception they all said that they preferred a smack to being sent to their room or having a treat withdrawn. They understood why they were smacked, and felt that the treatment helped them to change their behaviour and attitudes without damaging them. None of them had become aggressive or disturbed as a consequence of this caring physical correction. As with so many of God's perfect principles, this one has been so distorted that it is now in disrepute. Yet if it is applied in God's way, then only good results.

Attitudes not actions

This principle is closely linked with discipline, but can also be applied to other areas of family life. As the Bible points out, we are apt to be influenced by external appearances rather than the motives that drive them. It is important that in our parenting, we also look on the heart, as God does (1 Samuel 16:7). As has already been discussed, this helps us to distinguish between childish irresponsibility and deliberate defiance. Sometimes a child is genuinely innocent of any malicious intent when committing an apparently heinous crime. When my sister was very young she sat and watched my father work on the car. As he wrestled with some stubborn nuts under the chassis, she quietly and efficiently undid the jack and let the car down on top of him. Fortunately, he was not seriously hurt! Penny, though, had not meant to cause any harm, and was too young to foresee the consequences of her action. In that situation, she should not have been punished.

One of the respondents to the questionnaire recalls how Philip, her three-year-old, made a 'cake' out of rabbit food, soap powder and water on the dining room floor. This occurred while his mother was marooned on the loo, blissfully unaware of the mess that awaited her downstairs. Again, although the results of his actions were extremely visible and dramatic, his underlying attitude was innocent, and therefore he could not be punished for what he had done, just warned not to do it again!

There are other times when you might ask your child to do something to help and half an hour later, the job still has not been done. You need to discern whether the excuse of memory lapse is genuine or not. If the child really was so immersed in his activity that your request slipped his mind, then it is not fair to do more than remind him again, whereas a wilful decision to ignore the demand would result in a more stringent response. It is easy to define a child from his behaviour, but sometimes we are mistaken in our interpretation. We assign them motives that they do not have, and treat them accordingly. This often occurs when children are quarrelling and we attempt to arbitrate. We deal with the behaviour rather than the attitudes underlying it.

Likewise, we may be concerned by our child's schoolwork. Is he not trying, is there a problem, or have we overestimated his abilities? If his attitude is good and he is doing his best, then we cannot ask more of him, nor can we make him feel responsible for the perceived failure. It is all a matter of knowing your child and the impulses driving him.

Making the child feel special

Everyone needs to know that they are of individual value and unique worth. Many problems in adulthood arise out of a sense of worthlessness. One of our tasks as parents is to instil a knowledge of their own value into our children. This is quite a challenge, especially if you have a large family. There is a tendency, however much we fight against it, to treat them as a group and not sufficiently emphasise their individuality. We have found, though, that it takes comparatively little endeavour on our part to have an extremely beneficial effect on the children. Small gestures from us can make all the difference to the child;

- **Eye contact**. Looking the child in the eye as you listen or speak to him is an important signal. It tells him that he has your attention, and that what he says is important to you.

- **Individual time**. This is a primary cause of guilt for many parents. Graham and I spend most of our time with the family, yet still feel that we do not give enough time to each child individually. We plan special events with individual children, such as shopping trips, coffee in town, a walk with the dog, but inevitably these are spaced out among all the other demands on our time. What is more difficult is giving specific time every day to each member of the family. Yet very little of this individual time is required to make the child feel special. I often have one or other of the children helping me to prepare the evening meal, and this time can prove to be extremely valuable. Bedtimes are also important for giving the child personal attention. This is usually when our energy is at its lowest ebb and we long for a bit of peace and quiet, but it is also the best opportunity to concentrate on a child individually. If some of them share rooms, allocate different bedtimes so that they each have some time alone with you.

- **Enter their world**. Seeing things from the child's perspective is a good way of making him feel special. Instead of dismissing some of their games as silly, join in once in a while. Recall your own childhood, and your reactions then, and don't always expect adult responses. Instead, relate to them at their own level, without being patronising. It's amazing how much fun we can have when we let ourselves be children again for a little while!

In Titus, Paul writes of what is expected of an elder, and his reference to the family could serve as a summary for all Christian parents, not just elders: '*An elder must be blameless, the husband of but one wife, a man whose children believe and are not open to the charge of being wild and disobedient*' (Titus 1:6). While we are all thinking of the many times when our children are open to the charge of being wild and disobedient, it is good to remember that it is God who supplies us with everything we need for life and godliness (2 Peter 1:3). He gives us the power to deal with the responsibility he has given us.

6

Let Him who has Ears to Hear . . . (Simeon – Listening)

*Everyone should be quick to listen, slow to speak, and slow
to become angry.*
(James 1:19)

Our house is a very noisy one. Shouts, laughter, yells, singing,
barks, television, tape recorder, computer, piano, drums . . . all
compete for air time, and the golden sound of silence is rarely
present except in late evening. (And then the hamster starts
up!) With all this noise and the perceived need to 'get your say
in', there is a great danger that the art of listening will be
severely neglected. This is especially apparent at mealtimes,
when Graham and I sometimes feel that we have spent the
entire meal on a crowd-control exercise. *If* they take notice of
our injunction for only one person to be speaking at once, it is
obvious that they are using that person's turn to rehearse what
they will say next, rather than listening and responding, and
then rush to be the next to speak, as soon as, or sometimes
before, the previous person has finished! Visitors who have few
or no children often come away shell-shocked!

It was while delivering one of my impromptu mealtime
lectures, this one on the subject of listening and taking an
interest in each other's conversation, that it occurred to me

that parents too can be in danger of losing their capacity to listen to (as opposed to hearing) their children. We have so much to say to them that we can become focused on the one-way communication of us to them. Of course, we do listen to them, but we can become so used to the chatter and sheer volume of their output that we respond with our minds elsewhere, already thinking of the next thing. Yet to listen properly to our children, to their underlying messages as well as what they appear to be saying, is a vital parenting skill and can prove utterly invaluable during the communication black-out of the teenage years.

God is a speaking God, and throughout Scripture there are exhortations to listen to him. It becomes increasingly obvious that he rates the skill of listening very highly. The Bible is littered with 'stubborn and stiff-necked' people who fell by the wayside because they refused to listen. The book of Proverbs is full of commands to listen: *'Listen, my son, to your father's instruction and do not forsake your mother's teaching'* (Proverbs 1:8), and *'he who answers before listening – that is his folly and his shame'* (Proverbs 18:13). As a young boy, Jesus listened to his teachers (Luke 2:46) and was himself very good at listening to people and interpreting their underlying messages. He often urged his followers to listen to him: *'Jesus called the crowd to him and said, "Listen and understand" '* (Matthew 15:10), *'My sheep listen to my voice; I know them, and they follow me'* (John 10:27).

If, therefore, the Lord places such emphasis on the art of listening, it is important for us, as his followers, to develop it. As with any other godly characteristic which we hope to expand in our lives, it is comforting to know that God gives us the means to do it. As we spend time in his presence and learn to hear his voice, we will find that it becomes increasingly easy to listen, not only to him, but also to those with whom we have contact.

Listen to your child

This might seem so obvious that you are tempted to skip the paragraph altogether, but as I suggested earlier, we might not listen as well as we think we do. Consider Steve and Lynne, who, while camping at a Bible Week, did not listen properly to their little girl. Ruth, their eleven-month-old, was put to bed in her travel cot in the tent and was sleeping peacefully when they went to bed. In the early hours of the morning, they heard a child crying in the distance. This went on for over ten minutes, until Lynne suddenly said, 'You know, that sounds like Ruth.' They rushed to check the travel cot and, sure enough, it was empty. She had climbed out (a first), unzipped both her inner tent and the outer tent and crawled about two hundred yards before deciding that it wasn't such a good idea after all.

A humorous example of not listening, but I confess that there are times, such as serving up a meal, or when there are lots of people around, or, if I'm honest, when I'm just plain tired, when I hear what the children are saying and answer after a fashion, but I am not really listening. At such times, I might not look at them as they talk, because I am continuing with another activity, and I am somewhat mechanical in my replies. I might even interrupt by saying something to someone else. These are not good listening techniques, and can make the children feel insignificant or unvalued. Listening means more than hearing the words spoken; it is an interactive activity, which can teach you a lot about the person you are listening to. Of course, children often want to talk to us at the most inappropriate moments, when we really cannot listen, but even then it is important to show that we value what they have to say, though they might have to wait to say it.

Listen to learn

As your child grows older he will develop his own ideas and opinions, and become more and more a separate personality. It is pleasurable as well as valuable to spend time getting to know him as you would an adult. Children can become real pals as they grow up, and as with any other friendship it is good to find out about their thoughts and views. Discover more about your child's character and personality by listening to his opinions on events and circumstances. You may be amazed at some of the things he comes out with, because you may not have actually been listening to him for a while.

Keep in touch with his life as he grows older by listening to his talk about school, friends, sports, music. Our oldest son, Simeon, has developed a real love of history, and enjoys talking about the Second World War. We have had some absorbing discussions on the subject. Joel, our second child, is interested in maps and all things geographical, and will spend ages poring over a map, asking questions and suggesting ideas. It is fascinating to listen to them and to learn more of their personalities through their interests.

Learning about school is important, as it occupies such a large part of their lives. The majority of their time during a school term is spent away from us, and often we do not have the faintest clue what they get up to. When I was a teacher, I was surprised at the number of people who did not recognise their child from my description of his behaviour and personality. 'Well, he's not at all like that at home,' was the invariable response. This seemed to apply whether the comments were positive or negative! I have since said similar things to my children's teachers! Once we accept that teachers are on our side, then their observations and support can be very helpful.

So it is good to learn more about your children by encouraging them to talk about what they do at school, the things they are studying, their friends, what happens at playtimes and how they feel generally about school. A good tip is to ask open-ended questions rather than ones which only require the grunted 'yes' or 'no'! I'm not suggesting that you subject your child to the Inquisition the minute he walks through the door, but engaging him in conversation at various times about his school day is valuable, and interesting as well. You will find out so much by taking note of comments he makes, either directly to you or to other children in your hearing. Listening to children's conversations can be very illuminating; their attitudes to other adults, friends and activities are revealed, and you certainly feel that you are getting to know your child in a much deeper way. As BT keep telling us, 'It's good to talk,' but it's good to listen as well!

It is also an education in another form, for not only do you learn more about your child, but you gain information about all sorts of facts which might otherwise have escaped your notice. I now know about various pop groups, the merits of different brands of trainers, the rules of offside, and the meaning of words such as 'pagger' ('to hurt a great deal') and 'done with' ('told off'). Like it or not, your children are part of the youth culture, and you can discover much about it by listening to them. If we don't learn about our children and the world they inhabit, we are in danger of being sidelined as irrelevant and out of touch as they get older.

Listen to love

The art of empathic listening: this means putting yourself in the shoes of the one to whom you are listening. It means understanding and identifying with the feelings expressed. Sometimes, the trigger of the feelings might seem trivial to us, but it is vital to hear the child out, because often there is an underlying reason for their outburst. Recently, Barnaby over-reacted to a small irritation from one of his brothers. When we reproved him for talking so rudely, he burst into tears and rushed upstairs, shrieking that no one liked him. We looked at each other in bewilderment. What was going on? After allowing him time to calm down a little, I went to talk to him. At first, he only spoke about the incident which had triggered the event, even though it was an unintentional annoyance on his brother's part. He would not accept this, and felt aggrieved that he had been rebuked. 'And anyway,' he said, 'no one likes me at school. They all pick on me because of my teeth.' And there at last was the true cause of all this emotion. By talking things through, we were able to ascertain exactly what the problem was, and he was able to acknowledge that maybe things weren't quite as bad as he thought. I helped him to rationalise the hurt, and assured him again of our love for him. Without being asked, he apologised for his earlier rudeness, and the incident was over. By listening to him, sharing in his feelings, and showing that I understood, I was able to help him deal positively with the situation.

Showing that you are listening affirms children and expresses love to them. There is a security in knowing that there is someone who will hear, accept and value what they have to say. With peers and even siblings, the child can feel vulnerable about allowing too much of himself to be exposed. If he ventures an opinion or an emotion, there is a real danger of it being ridiculed or dismissed. Children's feelings can be lacerated by the casual cruelty of their peers and they often protect themselves with a veneer of indifference or flippancy. So it is important that at home they will be listened to in a positive manner. Encourage your child to express himself fully, without interruption, and reflect back what he has said, to ensure that you have really understood. A good way to do this is to begin, 'So what you're saying is . . .' followed by a summary of what you perceive to be the issue. Often, he will need to restate what he has said if you have not thoroughly comprehended. This is especially important in times when the child is feeling strong emotion. Much patience is needed, but it is important to show that you identify with his feelings and help him to talk through the causes. Tell him about episodes in your own life when you felt the same, and how you coped. This will demonstrate to him that you do indeed understand, and that he is not the only one to be in such a situation.

Empathic listening helps the child to grow in confidence and self-esteem. Our children need to know that if they have a problem (or conversely something intensely exciting to communicate) they can come to us and we will help them to come to terms with all they are experiencing, that they will be understood, accepted and supported in whatever they are undergoing. Because we look at their circumstances with all the benefit of adult hindsight, we can sometimes give the impression that their traumas or thrills are insignificant. Avoid this impression at all costs, because it is a real obstacle to communication. The child will not feel as free another time to talk to you about what is on his mind, and a pattern of silence will be established. Whenever possible, we need to listen with our heart and spirit as well as with our ears.

Listen to the unspoken

Simeon came home from school the other day, and one look at his face told me that something was wrong. He gave me his usual hug, and when asked if he had had a good day replied with an affirmative grunt. My questions about various lessons and friends received reasonably positive answers and, on the strength of those, I might have thought that all was well. Yet his shoulders were drooping, and there was an anxious look on his face. Closing the door on the rest of the family, I probed a little deeper and discovered that he had received a detention for handing in some work late ('but I didn't *know* . . .') and was very upset about it. He had felt too ashamed to tell me, but having been encouraged to do so was relieved to be able to talk about it. I was able to listen and comfort, as well as gently drawing a lesson from the whole incident.

There are many times when silences speak louder than words, when what is left out of an account is more significant than what is left in. Is your child omitting to talk about certain subjects? This could, of course, merely mean that other topics have taken priority, or it could indicate a problem area. Telling only half a story could mean that there is trouble in some area of his life – school, perhaps, or friendships. It is important to take note of the silences and, in as diplomatic a way as possible, investigate them. Very often, a child is longing to tell you what is on his mind but is not sure how to go about it. While we don't want to intrude on their privacy, it is always worth attempting to break through the silences, particularly if the child is normally quite talkative.

Notice also body language. We have all had the experience of the child who says 'sorry' when told to do so, but whose folded arms, clenched fists and drawn brows are saying something very different! A child's real feelings are often expressed in his posture, facial expressions and the spring, or lack of it, in his step, whatever words he might use. It's understandable to feel frustrated and rejected when he won't communicate anything of meaning to you, but allow him to go at his own pace. Approach any potential problem area obliquely, leaving lots of opportunities for him to respond, in the hope that this will create a context for him to talk. Don't 'bulldoze' your child into talking to you by bombarding him with questions followed up by reproaches, such as 'You used to be such a chatty little boy; you never seem to want to talk to me these days,' but, by being around, signal your willingness and desire to listen to whatever he chooses to talk about. My experience is that these occasions are usually at the most inconvenient times, when one is just about to go out, or late at night, when tiredness is the overwhelming sensation. But it is vital at those times when your child chooses to open up that you give him your full attention and listen. The opportunity might not appear again for a long time.

Teach your child to listen

Unlike talking, listening does not seem to come easily to children! The best way to encourage a child to listen is to be a good listener. The child will learn by example. This principle is fine in theory, but unfortunately not always so simple in practice. Even if you are a very good listener, it will still take your child a long time to master the art. Yet it is so important that they do learn, as learning to listen is part of their progress away from childish self-centredness towards empathy and a selfless attitude towards others. Moreover, a child who cannot listen will have educational problems, as he fails to absorb what is being taught, and lacks concentration to apply it anyway.

Stop interrupting!

It *is* possible to train your child out of this habit! Many adults have not learnt the lesson, and it arises from being more interested in your own thoughts and opinions than in the person's with whom you are speaking. In our household, Robert particularly has an interrupting problem (or should I say that *we* have his interrupting problem; it isn't a problem to him!). He speaks as soon as he thinks – before that, sometimes – and frequently bursts into a room, already in full flow. At school, he inserts himself between the teacher and whoever she is speaking to in order to be heard. Sometimes, one's instinctive reaction to this type of behaviour does not always constitute best childcare practice!

Make it a policy not to allow children to interrupt already

ongoing conversations, but likewise ensure that you do not interrupt *their* conversations. A few months ago, I noticed to my dismay that I had got into a very bad habit of interrupting the children, usually to issue an instruction to someone else. Someone would be trying to tell me something, and I would nod to show I was listening, but then suddenly say, 'Nathanael, put that down *now*,' or 'Just move that over here, will you, please.' (Joyce Grenfell, eat your heart out!) I felt dreadful, because it was sending such unintentionally bad messages to the children. Since then, I have worked much harder to listen properly!

It is important not to undermine the child when stopping him from interrupting. Make it clear that you are interested in what he has to say, but that he must wait to say it. With older children, you can also explain that it can be hurtful to interrupt people, as if you are not interested in them. Sometimes, when we are all together, the children interrupt each other and me constantly. When it happens to me, I stop and refuse to continue with what I was saying. This is usually very effective, and they all apologise and beg me to continue. The impact of this method is somewhat spoiled if what you have to say is completely mundane: 'What I was *going* to say was that your bedrooms need tidying'!

Encourage debate

As the children have grown older and a little more mature, we have enjoyed having discussions about a wide variety of topics, some of them domestic or personal, such as who will have which bedroom, favourite subjects at school or our holiday plans, and some of them more general such as topical news items, pollution, bullying, advertising or Princess Diana. Often, the children have set views, picked up at school, or else they give a 'knee jerk' reaction to the debate, and it has been valuable to present another perspective and assist them to think arguments through. A friend of mine had this experience recently when her six-year-old daughter made an exclamation of distaste when two African ladies appeared on television. Shocked, because they are not in any way a racist family, Zoe asked her what she meant by the exclamation. 'It's because they are so black,' said the little girl, who does not rate black as one of her favourite colours. Zoe was able to use the opportunity to have a good discussion with her daughter and older sons about race relations and the essential equality of all before God!

There are many occasions when an incident, news item or television programme can provide the basis for a lively debate. We try not to influence the children too much with our own opinions, but ask them leading questions and show them that every argument has two sides. Sometimes we use the 'circle time' method, described in Chapter 3. To recap, a certain subject is under discussion and a small object is introduced without which you cannot speak. Each person has the object in turn, and when it is your turn, you can have your say uninterrupted, and also comment on what other people have contributed. In this way, the children learn to listen to each other, and assimilate points of view which are not necessarily their own. They love the importance of giving their opinion and the value that is put upon the discussion as a whole.

Direct conversations

Occasionally it is necessary to be quite interventionist when children are talking. Obviously, when they are small they chatter away in a stream of consciousness that James Joyce would have been proud of, but as they get a little older, the parent almost instinctively begins to direct their talk, so that they increase their vocabulary and learn new facts about the world around them. 'Look! Car!' the child will say, wanting to communicate.

'Yes, it's a red car, isn't it? Look at its shiny wheels. I wonder where it is going?' the parent might reply. Without realising it, she is teaching the child how to make conversation. This directing can also teach them how to listen.

If we have visitors for a meal, I usually make a few suggestions to the boys as to how they might make conversation, not because I am trying to make a good impression (honest!) but because I am trying to teach them how to make people feel welcome and how to take an interest in others. My thesis to the children goes something like this: we are fortunate to have Hannah with us, we could benefit from her being with us, and we want her to benefit from being with us; we can talk about the merits of Man United or tell silly jokes at any time, when Hannah is not with us. The boys take it on board for a while, and politely ask Hannah about her day or job and then gradually revert to their football-speak – but at least they tried!

Some people might think that such guiding of children in what they say is too contrived and that they should be natural, and I accept that argument as valid. Nevertheless, I think that conversation is a skill which needs to be learned as much as any other skill which we teach our children. As long as they are allowed space to communicate in their own way, a small amount of direction in their discourse can prove very helpful. Too many adults are unable to communicate comfortably with each other because they were never shown how to in their formative years.

Distinguishing different voices

There are so many different voices clamouring for your child's attention as he matures – yours, his friends', the media, advertising, God's. It is hard for him to know which ones to listen to. At school, he will hear different facts put forward as truth, and those which you have taught him belittled as falsehood. Throughout his early life, yours has been the dominant voice. Now, there are many others, and he has to learn to discriminate and decide for himself which ones are worth listening to. It astonishes me how many people believe all that newspapers or television say without question.

Try to help your child to recognise that all voices, including your own, have a personal bias, a specific purpose in speaking. Some are good, some not so good. Discuss what those purposes might be, and whether we agree with them. This will help him to decide what he wants to listen to and what he wants to ignore. The attractiveness of some voices is hard to withstand; their very difference from what the child is used to acts as a magnet. Children love excitement, action, noise, speed, change. They will want to listen to voices which entice them towards these things. Of themselves, these voices are often not wrong, but it is our task to help our children to think carefully about what they hear and weigh up how much they should take on board.

Listen to your own words!

It is an important part of listening to consider what we say before we say it, and the effect it might have. If we have not been sensitive to what the other person has been saying, then we might easily say something to hurt or offend. In their immaturity, children often 'put their foot in it', and usually no one minds, because it is amusing childishness rather than malicious intent. However, there is no harm in beginning to teach your children to think about what they are saying and to whom they are saying it.

The other week, my friend Heather called in when the children were at home. The children are very fond of her, and stayed chatting with her while we all had a drink. They asked questions about her new baby, due in about two months' time.

'Our teacher was expecting a baby,' said Nathanael, 'but it died in her tummy.' There was a bit of a silence as we all digested the implications of his words, and the older boys looked rather uncomfortable. Heather took it in her stride, but without getting cross or accusing I took the opportunity to point out that it wasn't really a good idea to tell a lady with a baby in her tummy about another baby who had died. It might make her upset or nervous about her own baby. Nathanael understood what I meant and gave Heather a big hug to make up for it. Hopefully, all the boys learnt something from the incident.

Sometimes, though, children do need a sharper reminder to think of what they are saying. They are capable of saying extremely cruel things to each other, not really caring what effect their words have on their hearers. They have not learnt to put themselves in another person's place. Teaching the child to listen to his own words and consider them is very much a part of the process.

Listening to God

In the midst of it all, encourage your child to hear God for himself. If he can listen to God then he has a foundation for the future. It is not always easy for children to have a consistent relationship with the Lord, but they are often the most sensitive to the word of God, and the least cluttered by intellectual and emotional obstacles. It is important that we assist them to read the Bible and pray regularly. There are many excellent study aids for children which make Bible reading and prayer fun and meaningful activities. Encourage the children to expect God to speak to them when they are reading the Bible or praying or at any other time in their lives. Tell them how you listen to God, and the various situations through which he has spoken to you. They love to hear stories of your past, and talking about your adventures of faith will give their own relationship with God a boost. It will also give them confidence to share what they have heard from God with you and with the church family during a Sunday meeting or church youth group. With a Christian peer group as well as Christian family life, the voice they listen to most will, hopefully, be the Lord's.

I have a friend who rarely really listens to me. She asks questions, but then interrupts as I am answering her. She then asks the same questions again some time later, showing that she did not take in what I said the first time. Often, when I am talking, she nods and murmurs agreement, but her eyes show that her mind is elsewhere. This is proved when she starts off on a completely different tack as soon as I stop. The effect this has on me is to make me feel insignificant and unvalued. I also fear that I must be very boring and therefore inadequate. My friend would not want me to feel like that and has no unkind intention in her inattention, but the effect is there anyway. I'm sure that we have all had similar experiences at some point in our lives. Let's ensure that we do not inadvertently have the same effect on our children, or allow them to grow up making others feel undervalued or inadequate. Good listening skills enrich the listened to and the listener alike!

7

Instructed Ears!

The sovereign LORD has given me an instructed tongue,
to know the word that sustains the weary.
He wakens me morning by morning,
wakens my ear to listen like one being taught.
(Isaiah 50:4)

Listen to each other

When God created humankind he commented that it is not good for man to be alone. The comment could apply especially to parenthood! As I have said elsewhere, I appreciate that there are many parents who, through various circumstances, are forced to 'go it alone' and who work very hard at it, but they would probably be the first to say that it is not the ideal. Indeed, one of the respondents to my questionnaire observed: 'As I am now a single parent, I find all the decisions I have to make alone very demanding.' Others have spoken to me of the burden of unshared responsibility, and the unsatisfied need for individual space.

God designed parenting as a two-person job, and that does not just mean two people living in the same house. There are many women (and some men) who, though married, are essentially lone parents. The partner works long hours, leaving early in the morning and often not returning until the children

114

are asleep. At weekends, he is either catching up on chores or too exhausted to give much time to the family. I have a friend with a large number of children whose husband retrained as a doctor (even though he was doing well in his previous job), and who is now working the appalling hours of the junior hospital doctor. The children rarely see him, and though he would say that he was doing all this for the family's sake, one has to wonder whether he has his priorities right. Of course, work and career are very important, in terms of both providing an income and personal fulfilment, but don't let them take precedence over the children's deepest needs. If it is at all possible, aim for the ideal of both parents being deeply involved in every aspect of their children's upbringing. A vital part of this involvement is communicating, talking and listening to each other about the children.

Share your feelings

Have you ever had the sort of day with the children when nothing seems to have gone right? When you lurched from one crisis to another, or dealt with several simultaneously? The baby won't feed, and then is sick all over you ('I shouldn't have eaten lentils last night'). At the same time, the toddler misses the potty (deliberately? is she demonstrating insecurity?), and the phone rings, with your bright, energetic single friend on the other end ('We *were* at university together, weren't we?'). It takes half an hour to clear up the mess, and another half hour to get ready to go out. If the rest of the day follows the same pattern – and it usually does – you are at the end of your physical and emotional tether by the time your partner arrives home in the evening. Although you don't want to submerge him in gruesome, negative facts the minute he steps through the door, it is good, at an appropriate time, to be able to talk to him about what has gone on, and the feelings arising from it all. Likewise, he might have had a stressful day, and may find the transition from work to home quite difficult. He loves and enjoys family and job, but balancing the demands of employer, children, spouse, to say nothing of church and friends, is not easy. There is always that sneaking feeling that more could be done in every department.

Or you both might be out all day in paid employment, and when you return it is to find that the washing machine has flooded during the day, your eldest was involved in a fight at school, and your youngest, for some indefinable reason, is in a vile mood and keeps snapping at everyone. The meal burns and you have run out of so much that a trip to the supermarket seems inevitable. Everyone wants help with their homework, and in the middle of it all the dog is sick in the kitchen. It is at times like these that you need to offload your feelings on to a sympathetic shoulder!

Parenting is a very vulnerable job, with a high 'perceived failure' factor, and it is vital that you can express your feelings about situations, individuals, strategies and performance to your partner. Talking and listening releases tension and brings things back into perspective again. If you are a lone parent, try to develop a relationship with someone, a close friend or relative, with whom you can talk things over. Be honest about mistakes and about your emotions towards the children.

Feelings are a volatile indicator of true success, and should not be trusted. For instance, as your child goes through various 'phases' (mine are always going through some phase or other!) it is possible that you will not like them very much. This in no way affects your love for them, but if you confuse feelings for the true commitment of love, then you might fear that you do not love them any more. This is not the case. Love is a constant decision of the will, a covenant, whereas emotions change in response to specific circumstances. You may feel alienated towards the person your child has temporarily become, but never show this dislike; it is, after all, directed towards the child's behaviour, not his person. Continue to express love to him, while making it clear that the behaviour is unacceptable, and talk through your feelings in private with your partner and with the Lord.

Listen to each other, empathise and then encourage, so that as you share your innermost souls you will help each other to develop as people as well as parents. It is all too easy to allow the concerns and stresses of parenthood to drive you apart rather than bring you closer. When you are tired and frustrated, a natural but unwise reaction is to snap at your spouse or blame him for the cause of your frustration. The children are being difficult, and your husband makes a suggestion, perhaps not as well timed as it could be, which is supposed to help. You, receiving it as implied criticism of the way you are handling things, retort angrily, and counter with a direct criticism of your own.

I'm sure that we have all been guilty of such behaviour at some time or other. If it does happen, ensure that you put things right as soon as possible, and continue the discussion away from the children. If I do have a disagreement with Graham in the children's hearing, I usually apologise to them (when I have regained my composure!) and reassure them that we still love each other. If appropriate, we will ask them to apologise for their part in the incident. How much better it is, though, when we are able to have a mutual exchange of our inner thoughts and emotions in a peaceful and supportive atmosphere! (It can happen!) By sharing your feelings about the children and about your abilities as a parent, you are able to help each other succeed in the awesome task of raising a family. One means of access to God's power for parenting is through each other, and we need to be aware of and protect this valuable channel of communication.

Communicate positives as well as negatives

Somehow, the bad behaviour and attitudes of your little darlings seem to stick in the memory far more than their kind actions and obedience! 'Guess what she's done *now*!' is usually not a lead-up to a description of your child playing happily with her sister. There is a tendency to spend more time discussing the problem areas of family life than dwelling on the good bits! Obviously, as mentioned in the paragraph above, there is an ongoing need to talk about the pressure points, but as a balance to this make a decisive effort to articulate all the positive attributes and conduct of your children.

Tell each other the good things you have experienced with your child: the achievements, the kind act, the cute saying, the improvement in behaviour. This will encourage you and also create a better context within which to deal with the negatives. Get into the habit of viewing your child in a positive light; if necessary, be deliberate in listing her good qualities to each other. Otherwise, there is a danger of becoming over-critical.

Listen to your partner's views on the children, and learn from them. Your children will have elements of both your characters in them, and so you are more likely to identify with some aspects of their personalities than others. Together, you can have a more complete approach to the complex being you have created. It is so valuable to gain a contrasting perspective on responses and character which are strange to you. For instance, I find I have an instinctive understanding of Barnaby because he is so similar to me in temperament, while Graham often finds his behaviour totally perplexing (and, therefore, by deduction, mine also! Oh dear!). On the other hand, he is able to offer insight into the more reserved, cautious character of Joel, whose reactions sometimes mystify me. Together we understand them in a way that we would not apart.

Be consistent in policies

We have all seen the child who, having been refused a sweet or some other treat by Mummy, sets off to ask Daddy the same request. If Daddy is on his toes, he will first check whether Mummy has already been asked. If he isn't, then he may well assent to the request, thus unintentionally undermining Mummy's authority. The worst scenario is if Daddy knows that Mummy has said no, and for some reason of his own says yes anyway. The child, in the short term anyway, is on to a winner. The latter situation happens quite frequently when parents are divorced or at odds with each other, and the child can play one off against the other to his seeming advantage. Such inconsistencies, and others, such as what constitutes acceptable behaviour and what does not, can create great instability in a family. If one parent allows a child to answer back, for instance, and the other pulls him up for it, then dual standards are in operation. The child begins to distance himself from the stricter parent, yet does not respect the other. Children need secure boundaries in order to thrive. They become confused and unsure of themselves if the boundary posts are constantly moved backwards and forwards.

Talk through any decisions regarding behaviour, discipline, specific situations or general strategies before they arise, if possible. It is a good idea to be thinking about potential issues ahead of time, and learning all you can about them. If I was going into any other job, I would train and study, perhaps for years, and so it is not unreasonable to prepare and educate myself for this most important job of all. Otherwise, I am caught 'on the hop', unsure how to deal with situations as they arise, and reacting, not always wisely, to circumstances rather than to a well-thought-out policy which will benefit our children. There are plenty of resources available to give you a foundation for your own thoughts and decisions. I have read numerous books on all aspects of childcare ('No, I'm sorry darling, I can't play with you now; I'm reading a book on parenting'!) as well as going on parenting seminars. Care for the Family run excellent courses nationwide. There are even web sites on the Internet, if you're electronically minded, dedicated to children and child-care. Focus on the Family – http://www.fotf.org – is a good place to start! All this plus the Bible, which is a handbook for parenting, will help you both to make informed decisions as to how you are going to bring up your children.

Try not to argue in front of the children about how a situation should be handled. It can make them very insecure, or else they will take advantage of the division in the ranks to press for their own way, thus adding to the stress of the moment. I have been very grateful to Graham for the times he has bitten his tongue when he has disagreed with my impetuous decisions and waited for a quiet moment to discuss them. Don't be afraid to say to the children, 'I can't make a decision right now, I'm afraid. I'll talk it through with Daddy/Mummy first.' Listen to each other's views on things.

It is surprising how different expectations can be, depending on your own childhood. You might have very definite views about diet or television or the way Christmas should be cele-brated, and then discover to your astonishment that your spouse doesn't think that way at all! For instance, my sisters and I were brought up in a household where the television was never on during the day. Our father had no interest in sport and would not have dreamt of watching a televised football match. My sister has married a keen sports follower, whose idea of relaxation is to sit in front of the football or rugby on a Saturday or Sunday afternoon. At first, she found this quite hard to come to terms with, especially when the children wanted to join him. Eventually, she realised that she had to accept that his expectations were as valid as hers, and they came to a compromise on how weekend sports television could be balanced with other activities.

Once decisions have been arrived at and policies put in place, for example concerning how and when to discipline, then it is vital that you are consistent in those decisions. Children are very quick to pursue any weakness in the parental authority which they may see as to their advantage. As has been mentioned before, playing one parent off against the other is an ancient game, especially popular among children of separated parents, but it does not contribute to stable family life and is therefore to be avoided. Have a strategy and then stick to it, and back each other up in it. There have been times when Graham and I have not agreed about how a dispute should be resolved, but we always support the one involved in the decision-making. If we really feel strongly that the other has got it wrong, then we talk about it privately and are not afraid to go back to the children and admit that we have made a mistake, explaining how it came about.

When there is a consistency in our policies, the children know where they stand, and that helps them moderate their own behaviour. They know that disobedience will always be punished, that lying is totally unacceptable, that answering back will result in being sent out of the room, and that kindness to one another is what is expected of them. Such a framework, as long as it is not too overburdened with trivial rules and regulations, provides a security and a reference point for them. God, who gives us only what is for our best, provides clear and firm guidelines for living, and he requires that we do the same for our children.

Listen to others?

No!

When you first have a baby, it seems as if the whole world has a word of advice for you. The surprising thing is that most of the advice seems to conflict with itself, and you are left feeling confused and often inadequate as you learn how to cope with this vulnerable little person. My friend had a baby last year, and was having a bit of trouble breastfeeding. Even before she had left the hospital, she had been told a) to wake the baby regularly, b) to leave her to sleep, c) to use a nipple shield, d) not to use a nipple shield. When she got home, well-meaning friends contributed their own ideas and experiences, until in the end she was so confused that she almost gave in and took to the bottle! Because you are nervous and unsure of yourself in this thrilling but overawing new situation, you tend to assume that everyone must know more than you, and try to take on board all the advice you are proffered.

This abundance of counsel continues as your children grow. Everyone is a member of a family, and most people have their own children or know someone who has, and this seems to qualify them to offer opinions on every aspect of family life, from potty training to when to have the next one, from toddler tantrums to teenage tears. Mostly, this advice comes from a desire to help, but sometimes it can come from a judgmental attitude and can make the new parents feel deficient and even despairing. I can remember a friend of mine, mother of two quiet little girls, remarking, as I detailed another of Barnaby's outbursts, that she did not believe in the 'terrible twos'. The phrase was just an excuse for mismanagement of the child. She was not meaning to be unkind, merely stating an opinion, but I felt dreadful; a mixture of frustration, (because, without a doubt, he *was* going through the 'terrible twos'!) and self-condemnation, because I was obviously mismanaging him. I was quite glad when some years later, her third little girl proved to her beyond doubt that the 'terrible twos' did exist after all!

Listening too much to other people's beliefs, even if they are published in book form, can be unhelpful, if not actually damaging at times. As has been discussed before, it is wise to learn all that you can about this crucial job, just as you would for any other employment you undertake, but then it is important that you adapt the information you have gained to suit your own situation. Remain secure in what you have decided and don't be threatened when others proffer contradicting advice (even when it's your mother!).

It is especially vital to be aware of ideas and trends which might actually cut across biblical teaching. For instance, Dr Spock became a hugely popular parenting 'guru' in the late 1940s and 1950s, with his book *The Common Sense Book of Baby and Child Care* (1946). While many of his ideas were helpful and necessary, there were others which were not acceptable to Christians or others who questioned the long-term wisdom of his pronouncements. In a much-needed reaction to the rigid, affection-restricted childcare of the time, perhaps typified by the New Zealander Frederick Truby King, he went to the other extreme, advocating a completely child-led regime, interpreted, if not intended, as the child being allowed to do more or less what it wanted.

Truby King advocated a very strict routine in childcare:

> The normal baby should be fed only five times in the twenty-four hour day, at 6 a.m., 10 a.m., 2 p.m., 6 p.m., and 10 p.m. . . . The giving of food to a baby between 10 in the evening and six o'clock the next morning is a great mistake – it encourages an unnatural and bad habit . . . A baby cannot be expected to thrive if his mother is not regular and punctual in his daily routine. (Sir Frederick Truby King, *Feeding and Care of Baby*, extracted from *Motherhood from 1920 to the Present Day*, ed. Vivien Devlin, Polygon, 1995).

A whole generation of women brought their children up according to Truby King's rigid precepts. My own mother remembers having very little support from outside the family when she had me in the mid-1950s. She had not heard of Truby King, but said that she 'did have quite strict routines, with the babies being fed four hourly and everything else being done to a rigid timetable'. The prevailing childcare trend also included the idea that too much affection was bad for the baby – 'nothing should be allowed to excite or spoil babies; they were not to be given much love or attention' (Angela Holdsworth, *Out of the Doll's House*, extracted from *Motherhood from 1920 to the Present Day*). Such concepts appear alien to us today, and do not seem to line up with biblical teaching or parental instinct.

It is scarcely surprising that Dr Spock's book, with its emphasis on enjoying your baby and having fun, should be embraced so wholeheartedly. Unfortunately, his ideas caused people to move to the opposite extreme in their methods of parenting, almost denying the biblical concept of parental authority and discipline, and instead propagating the theory that the child must be allowed the freedom to do what he wants, because authority and restriction are bad for him and can impede his development into adulthood. One only has to look at the state of the family and society today to realise that the theory, while containing many nuggets of wisdom and truth, was essentially flawed. Even the good doctor himself has retracted some of what he has been alleged to have said in the light of succeeding changes in society.

Measure what you read, hear and observe about parenting against the word of God, which is the only absolute in a world where fashions in child-rearing are as ephemeral as fashions in clothing. Each trend has its good and bad points, and you will pick up much wisdom as you attempt to learn more about how to do your best in this difficult job. But don't be pressured into practices which you don't feel reflect God's ways.

Yes!

Of course it would be unwise never to listen to others. There are professionals, such as health visitors, doctors and childcare experts, who have much to offer us. Make use of their knowledge and experience, while still being aware that even the experts won't necessarily have exactly the right answers for your particular circumstances. Adapt what you learn to suit your own and your children's personalities and lifestyles. Listen also to what teachers and playgroup leaders have to say about your child. Children often behave quite differently when they are in another context, and you can learn a great deal by taking note of their teacher's comments.

There are times, for instance when you have tried *everything* and your baby is still crying, or when nothing that you say or do prevents confrontation with your teenager, when the wise advice of another parent or a good book can be a life saver. Graham and I have been helped immeasurably in our parenting by spending time with families whom we admire and would want to emulate. In particular, our friends Mel and Jean, who are a couple of stages ahead in their parenting journey, have taught us so much through conversation and example. From an early stage, I recognised an excellence in their parenting that I wanted to imitate in my own. As a young single, I lived with them for a while, when their children were pre-school, so I saw life in the raw! Though obviously there were times when Mel and Jean did not get it right, and times when they were utterly worn out with the whole thing, I realised then that the principles they were working by were holding strong and succeeding despite the mistakes.

Now, more years later than I care to admit, the children are young adults, warm, loving, enthusiastic people who relate well to their parents, other people and the Lord, and who have weathered the teen years remarkably smoothly. (In fact, Mel and Jean should be writing this book, not me!) I have learnt so much from spending time with them and asking them for the benefit of their experience when I have come up against problems with my own children. They have seen similar personality and behaviour patterns emerging in our children to their own, and have been able to encourage us that they will turn out OK after all and won't necessarily become the delinquents they seem to be heading for! And remembering back, I do recall that their children went through comparable phases and have now transformed into civilised beings!

All parents need a Mel and Jean. People who will help without being judgmental, who will make themselves vulnerable in order to share their family life with you. People to whom you can go when things are getting you down and will not think any the less of you for your temporarily negative thoughts. People who understand the pressures and joys of parenting because they have experienced the same, and who can point you in the right direction when you are feeling a little lost, because they have trodden the path ahead of you. And in your turn, you can become a Mel and Jean for someone else who is coming behind you!

Someone who is in the same position as you will give sympathy and understanding, but may not be able to help you to resolve your particular parenting problem, whereas someone who has reached a different point in their family life has more of an overview of your situation and can share some of the lessons they have learnt. Develop a friendship with people in the church whom you respect as godly parents, and don't be afraid to pump them for their opinions, ideas and guidance at every opportunity. They will probably be flattered to be asked, and certainly would not think of you as inadequate for asking.

We have also found it invaluable for the children to have other role models besides ourselves. Each of the boys has a special friend among the young people in the church, who spend time with them, having fun and encouraging them in their relationship with God and their relationship with their family. This is a situation which has evolved naturally, through the inspiration of Matt, the youth leader, who has a real vision for seeing children discipled by young people in the church as well as by their parents. How good for our teenager to see that Christians can be trendy, enjoy pop music and 'cool' clothes, and yet live pure lives, loving and worshipping the Lord. How wonderful for our volatile middle son to be invited out to tea on his own, and to spend time chatting and praying. And for Robert, so desperate to give and receive affection, it is marvellous to have someone visit him specially and play games with him.

Last Christmas, the children's ministry team each linked up with an individual child in the church, and undertook a project of the child's choosing, on the theme of giving. Barnaby and Matt made lots of cakes and then went in search of homeless people to give them to. Robert and Terri sorted through, cleaned and packed outgrown toys and sent them to his orphanage in Romania. Nathanael and Sam made presents and cards to send to a Japanese girl who became a Christian while in York and who is now back in Japan. Simeon and Cecily did a sponsored RSPCA dog walk and Joel made and sent cards to all the international students in the church, who would be far away from their families at Christmas. These activities, worthwhile and exciting in their own right, have an added value because they are at an individual level. Again, the children feel special and esteemed. The young people are working alongside us to reinforce and support our parenting aims.

We feel very happy to share our children with those whom we believe have a real care for them, and are happy to seek their advice and opinions on various aspects of the children's lives. They might not be parents, but they have taken the trouble to get to know our children and will see them from a different perspective to us. Likewise, there are times when the children might sometimes need an alternative input into a situation from that which we give them. We know we can trust these young people to give wise, biblical advice to the children as well as support and love. We also know that if they had any real concern about the children or the way we were handling a situation, they would feel able to come and discuss it with us.

Some parents might feel threatened by having other adults

so intimately involved with the family, feeling that somehow their own authority and standing might be undermined. I can identify with that insecurity, because there is always that lurking irrational fear that someone else (and in particular this helpful young person) could do a much better job of parenting your children than you can, but banish that thought – it's a lie – and encourage others to get involved with your children. We have found it to be a very positive experience. It is not a sign of inadequacy to allow others to help; it is part of God's plan. He wants the family of the church to 'bear one another's burdens' and that can apply as much to the happy burden of parental responsibility as to any other area of life. The children benefit greatly from the special attention they receive from someone they can look up to, and we benefit from the wisdom and practical help we are given.

Listen to the Lord

He is the most important one to listen to but, paradoxically, the one to whom we are frequently inattentive. Often in the busyness of family life, it is difficult to take the time listen to God. We rush around, firing questions, requests and complaints at him, and patiently he listens, understanding our situation. We grab a few minutes here and there to read the Bible, and we sit exhausted in the worship on a Sunday morning, grateful for some moments' peace. But we don't always listen to what the Lord has to say, which is a shame, because he has the wisest advice and the deepest allaying of our fears and guilt. Sometimes we don't want to listen, in case he says something we do not want to hear, but it is worth reminding ourselves that all he says is for our very best.

There are times, when you are very tired or 'low', when you can't even remember how to hear God. At those times it is good to listen to a worship tape and allow your spirit to be opened up to the Lord. Read 'easy' parts of Scripture, like the Psalms or the Gospels, and apply the words you read to your own life. You will be amazed how many of them are relevant! That is God speaking to you. In meetings, someone will say or pray something which could have been addressed directly to you. That is God speaking to you. Respond by acknowledging that you have heard, and ask him to help you live it out. He will. His Holy Spirit, gentle but powerful, will enable you to communicate with him and then to continue, with renewed strength, with the tasks he has given you to do.

God also has much to say in the crises of parenting. If one of your children has a physical, mental or spiritual problem, or if you have a problem with one of your children, take it first to God and find out what he has to say on the subject. Prayer is the first resource, not the last resort. I find myself spending a lot of needless time worrying about Simeon's susceptibility to peer pressure, or Barnaby's attitude towards his brothers, or some of the other myriad concerns which arise, *before* I pray about these things. Once I have talked with him, and listened for his response, I feel completely different about the issues, and am able to cope with them in a much better manner. Christians are not exempt from all the normal traumas of bringing up children but we have 'online' help, a loving Father who gives us the power to overcome the obstacles and become enriched by doing so.

Listen also to what God has to say to you and the family when there isn't a crisis, when things are going well and you are enjoying life. That is a good time to hear his thoughts on plans for the future and his encouragement about each of the children. He wants to speak to us at all times – just as we like to chat with our children – and not just when we need help. By praying, giving thanks, reading and thinking over sections of the Bible and worshipping alone and with the church, we will hear his voice more clearly and specifically as time goes on. Listening to and obeying his voice brings joy and excitement into the family, just as listening generally adds a depth and richness to life together.

8

Exceptional Courage Needed! (Barnaby – Encouragement)

Encourage one another daily, as long as it is called Today.
(Hebrews 3:13)

Our pastor, Mike, is fond of saying (usually in the middle of inspiring preaching!) that no one ever died of too much encouragement. Beneath the flippancy of the remark is a profound truth. To encourage means to impart courage, inspiration and resolution. It means to stimulate, motivate, animate, embolden, promote and cultivate. It's an impressive list, and flows off the tongue like poetry. Actually to *do* all those verbs is another matter though! Yet that is what is needed in order to fulfil our parental function. To be encouraged means to know that someone believes in you and is supporting you in all that you do and say. It is a vital element in parenting, for both parent and child, and without it much damage can occur. With it, your children will grow up secure and confident, and ready to pass on encouragement to others.

Encourage your child

Praise – a valuable teaching tool

We have recently had a new addition to the family – Charlie, an adolescent mongrel, late of the RSPCA home, affectionate, boisterous, energetic, eager to please and totally untrained. A bit like a young child, in fact! He is teachable, though, and slowly he is learning what he is and is not allowed to do, and to obey simple commands. The best way we have discovered to teach him obedience is to praise him in a very exaggerated manner. Every time he sits on command, we all chorus enthusiastically, '*Good* boy, Charlie, good *boy*. What a *clever* dog!' He wags his tail wildly, loving the fuss being made of him, and ready to reproduce any action which creates such pleasurable results.

Children, like dogs, have an inbuilt desire to please. They love to receive commendation for what they have done, and they will repeat behaviour which brings them affirmation. Sincere praise gives them a glow of self-worth which pervades their entire nature. Yet somehow, it is easier to remember to comment on the negatives of your child's behaviour than on the positives. Perhaps the positives are what we expect to be present in our child anyway, and so we take them for granted. We forget that children are on a steep learning curve, and need encouragement in areas which we would count as normal behaviour in adults. Whereas you would not say to an adult friend, 'Well done, you ate your food with your mouth closed just then,' or 'I really liked the way you spoke so kindly to Amy when she hurt herself,' it is necessary to do so for a child. Obviously, the manner in which we praise varies according to the age and maturity of the child, but they are never too old to be praised. We often forget, because we assume a level of behaviour which they have not yet completely attained.

Children will learn much more quickly what is acceptable

and 'right' if they are actively encouraged in it, rather than only discouraged in what is unacceptable and wrong. This applies as much, if not more, to teenagers as to toddlers. Praise is for actions and also attitudes. Compliment them on the pictures they paint or the work they have completed or the cake they have made, but remember also to praise your child for obeying immediately, or remembering to have the music at a tolerable level or being caring to a sibling or friend. In this way, their behaviour and thinking will be modified in a very positive way.

Encourage in weaknesses as well as in strengths

It is possible for a child to feel a failure even when being encouraged, if the encouragement is focused only on his strong points. He will begin to feel that he is only appreciated when he does well. If a child voices the opinion that he is no good at drawing, for example, a response might be, 'Well, you're very good at maths, aren't you? Look how well you did in that test.' The parent is trying to build up the child's confidence and encourage him in the things he is strong in, but is perceived by the child to be agreeing that he is no good at drawing, and that therefore there is no point in trying. Of course, this is not the case, but we can inadvertently send those signals if we do not also encourage him in the areas where he struggles.

To accept your weaknesses and remain secure is a hard lesson to learn and takes a long time. How many of us as adults find it difficult to admit that we are not very good at something? Therefore we must deal gently with our children as they discover where their strengths and weaknesses lie. It is difficult for them to cope with failure and we need to be sensitive to their vulnerability. This might be in an academic subject, or (more likely to damage self-esteem) in the sporting domain. Our boys, for example, love football. They know all about it, are enthusiastic supporters of one club or another, and keenly play every lunchtime at school. The trouble is, due to an unfortunate inheritance of genes, they are not very skilled at the game, though they try extremely hard. This matters a great deal in the cut and thrust of school life, where children do not mince their words. There have been many times when a crestfallen child, nearly in tears, has recounted how they have been called 'rubbish' or, worse still, not been allowed to play by some football baron. It's heartbreaking! The temptation is to tell them to turn their back on the whole thing and concentrate on the areas where they do excel. But this is not the answer, because they *want* to play football, and they want to be accepted as players. We have to assure them that they are competent players, that they are good sportsmen, they play well in a team, and that they are improving all the time. They need to accept that it is not their strongest talent and that other children are better, but, within that, they should be encouraged to be confident in their abilities.

Whatever your children do, there is always something you can find to encourage them with, even if, inwardly, you are disappointed with their performance or actions. Graham and I often say to our children that we don't mind where they come in competitive events, or whether they pass or fail exams, as long as they have done their best. That is a criterion that they understand and can work towards. I don't believe it is patronising or deceitful to say that, even though, of course, we are disappointed, deep inside, if our child fails at something. However, if we know that he has genuinely done his best, then it is crucial that we do not express that disappointment, but instead shower him with encouragement, bringing out the positives from the situation.

We also talk about the uniqueness of each person, how they each have different gifts, and tell them that it really is OK not to be as good at some things as you are at others. You are not a failure and you are not in competition with other children to be the best at everything. Do the best you can and enjoy it! This applies as much within the family as outside it. Trying to defuse sibling rivalry and assure each child that they are equally valued is one of a parent's biggest challenges! These are painful lessons to learn, and children absorb them much more easily if they are supported and motivated in every area, even in those very weaknesses with which they are struggling.

Enthuse your child!

'I'm bored' is the cry that every parent dreads. Their children have toys, games, activities, and yet they still come out with those annoying words. Parents feel a mixture of frustration, anger and bewilderment. What more can they do? Teenagers often consider that it is 'cool' to act bored or uninterested. Their parents produce what they believe to be a treat, only to be greeted with a raised eyebrow or a minimal grunt of thanks. Even those things in which they profess to be interested do not seem to cause much excitement.

Cultivating an enthusiastic attitude to life is an important part of our encouragement of our children. This attitude is as much caught as taught. If you yourself are enthusiastic about people, activities and events, then your children are likely to be so too. Sometimes, though, they need a little more guidance! Showing them how to express eagerness for activities or gratitude for a gift is helpful. Explain to them that people might feel hurt if it appears that their gift or presence is not really appreciated. Often, children are pleased with what is done for them or given to them, but just don't show it much. We need to encourage them to express their feelings in this instance! Another idea is to refuse to do something, such as arrange an expedition or some other treat, until a bit more enthusiasm is shown. Even comparatively mundane things can be approached enthusiastically if the children have been taught not to take anything for granted. In this country, most children live very comfortable lives. Without constantly reproaching them, it should be possible to make them aware of how fortunate they are to have houses to live in and more than enough food to eat and clothes to wear. The more enthusiastic a child is, the more pleasure he is likely to derive from life in general.

Dealing with fears

I was just drifting off to sleep when a horrible shriek jerked me awake. Leaping out of bed I rushed towards the source of the sound, convinced that someone was in serious pain. Nathanael, our philosophical, happy-go-lucky fourth child, was sitting up in bed sobbing. 'The school's burning down,' he kept repeating, as I hugged and calmed him. Although he went back to sleep straight away, the dream continued to haunt him over the next few weeks, and he was always talking about fire and things burning. We knew that his fears originated from the actual burning down of a school in York earlier that year, but we could not rationalise them away for him. The emotion was very real. We could only comfort him with the assurance that neither the school nor the house were likely to burn down, and pray with him.

Childhood is a place of extremes; excitement and happy adventure versus dark fears, where monsters, real and imagined, lurk in the unknown. As parents we need to help our children deal with the very genuine fears of childhood, encouraging them to face them rather than dismissing them as trivial or laughable. There are many anxieties which beset the child at different stages in his life: fear of pain, separation, disaster, loss, evil. Often, these are expressed as fear of the dark, or fear of water or dogs or going to strange places, or being without an adult. And children who have these fears manifest them in a huge variety of ways, such as disruptive behaviour, attention seeking, withdrawal, nightmares, or weepiness.

Parents are usually at a loss to know why their child has such fears, and what on earth to do about them.

Often, perhaps because it is quicker or more comfortable, we deal with the symptoms rather than the underlying problem. A nightlight will help the child who fears the dark, but don't then think the problem is solved. Telling the child that they are wrong or silly to be frightened might stop them talking about the fear, but it won't make it go away. Children often do not know how to articulate their fears, and it requires much patience (and sometimes the skill of a trained psychologist) to discover what is really troubling them.

Simeon appears to be confident, popular and successful at school, but every now and then, usually late at night when he can't sleep, he starts talking about his fears of forgetting his homework or being late or getting teased by the older children. The temptation is to jolly him out of such talk and tell him that he is being ridiculous to think in such a way.

Indeed there is sometimes a need to stop children wallowing in their emotions, because they can use them to manipulate the parents. My sister tells me that she is unsure whether to give in to her youngest child's demands to look in all the wardrobes and cupboards for 'gribleys' each night. Given that he always resists bedtime anyway, and uses every delaying tactic he can think of, she rather suspects that he is using his alleged anxiety as a way of putting off the evil hour of sleep! And yet, she wishes to allay any genuine fears he might have, by making him feel safe and secure. Not allowing children to dwell unduly on their fears is necessary, for their sakes as well as ours.

But it is also important to address in a serious manner the fears expressed, and find out what the fundamental difficulty is. Encourage the child to discover for himself the false assumptions in his fears, and help him to get to the real root of the issue. Make him state aloud the positive aspects of whatever is troubling him, so that he can feel better about it. And help him to pray about the problem, expecting God to answer. Pray with him, and for him, and having encouraged him in this way, help him to move forward in faith, not allowing him to repeat the fears ad infinitum, but instead to remind himself that they have been dealt with. This is imparting courage to him, and will become part of his thought patterns if consistently applied.

Above all, do not let your child give in to his fears, but help him to face them for what they are. I still have a very clear and painful memory of a trauma I went through at eleven years old. It was my first year at secondary school, and one day, I think because I wasn't well, I fainted in assembly. After that, I was terrified of fainting again. As soon as I stood in my place among the whole school, I was convinced that the room was going blurry and that I was losing consciousness. It got to a point when I was in hysterics every morning, shaking and frightened, begging to stay at home until assembly was over. (It was first thing in the morning, so this was a feasible option.) My mother, who had tried sympathetically to rationalise the situation with me, sometimes used to have to push me out of the door. I thought she was cruel and hard, because she wouldn't write and ask for me to be excused from assembly. Eventually, through being allowed to stay at the back of the hall for a while, I gradually overcame my fear. I look back now and realise that if Mum had given in, which I'm sure would have been the more pleasant option for her, I would have spent the rest of my life running away from fears. I am a highly strung person and even now get quite nervous before I have to do something difficult or unknown. If I hadn't learnt to conquer irrational fears at the age of eleven, I know that I would not have been able to face many of the things which have happened since in my life, and I would be the poorer for it. Thanks, Mum!

At the time, it seems kinder (and certainly easier) to let a child yield to his fears. Why force him to go swimming if he doesn't like it? Why make her go on a residential field trip if she gets nervous about it? Yet if we give in, there will be something else to contend with the next week or month, and each time the child becomes more gripped by that which he dreads. Helping our children deal with their fears, imparting courage to them, so that they can face their innermost uncertainties, is allowing their characters to flower in freedom. Once they realise that, with the help of the Holy Spirit, they can control their fear rather than letting it control them, then they are no longer held back from a full development of their potential. My prayer for my children is that they will be so secure in God and in themselves that they will never be held prisoner by the fears and doubts which can so easily hamper our lives as adults.

Envision your child

As has already been said, parenting is a long-term calling, and as parents we need to have a vision for our children's future. But it is good also to pass on that envisioning to our children. By this, I do not mean that we should pressurise them with our own desires and dreams for them. Of course we will have high hopes for our children, but to push them into one career, lifestyle or even marriage partner because it is our preference is wrong and damaging. It does happen. One hears of family businesses where it is always assumed that the son or daughter will carry on and no other options are really considered, or parents of one class who will not even contemplate sanctioning the marriage of their child to someone of a different class. Even if parents do not have their way in these matters, much long-lasting harm could be done. Graham and I need to be aware of the danger in this area ourselves, as we have already made it clear that we hope very much that the children will one day go to university. Yet they might not all want to, or be able to make that choice, and we must not make them feel that they have failed or disappointed us if they do something else. Having a vision and having dreams and expectations are subtly different things.

What I mean by envisioning your child is to open their minds and imaginations to the huge range of possibilities open to them in the present and the future. Teach them the reality of God's words in Jeremiah 29:11: ' *"For I know the plans I have for you," says the Lord . . .'* and that he wants them to have life and have it abundantly (John 10:10). Their future is in God's hands, and he has exciting prospects for them! Without getting too 'heavy', show them that life is precious and they need to make the most of it.

Although our children are still quite young, they are already thinking about what they might do when they grow up. Nathanael, for instance, has decided that he will either be a science teacher or a ball boy at Wimbledon! Simeon, on the other hand, is going to be a famous Hollywood actor. I'm sure we all remember deciding what we would be when we were 'grown-up'. Even though few of us ended up doing what we imagined, it was an enjoyable and valuable exercise, focusing our thoughts and imaginations on the future. While we don't want our children to wish away their childhood by constantly looking forward to when they are adults, it is useful to convey a sense of purpose and excitement about their futures.

Help them to identify their likes and dislikes in terms of academic, social and emotional spheres and then encourage them to develop these interests. Is your child of a scientific, analytical nature? Enable her to develop this characteristic. Or is she creative and good with her hands? Make sure that there are plenty of 'crafty' activities available so that she can experiment with various media. Perhaps one of your children is a computer wizard or very good at a particular sport. Take an interest in the work they are producing (quite difficult if you are not a computer wizard!) and do what you can to further them in it. This is not to say that they abandon those subjects which do not interest them as much, but that they spend extra time on those things which grip them. Sometimes, these interests are no more than a passing phase, to be replaced with something else equally fascinating. Sometimes, though, that early inclination which you encouraged develops into a career in later life.

It's strange how little we actually know about other people's jobs. I often wonder, 'What does he/she do all day?' I know what teachers or nurses or shop assistants do, but how do actuaries or chemical engineers or politicians actually fill their time? It's fascinating! (Perhaps that is why I like the 'Day in the life of . . .' features in magazines so much!) There is such a rich variety of careers and lifestyles available to our children, and they need to explore the possibilities before ever making a decision. Expose them from a young age to as many different ways of life and occupations as possible, so that they realise the potential before them. This does not necessarily mean organised tours to the local factory or newspaper printing press, though these would be fun things to do if it were practicable. Nor do you need to send for lots of brochures from careers offices. It is more a matter of observation as you travel about, watching television documentaries, and asking people who visit or who you meet about their jobs. In this way, the children have a much wider view of life choices.

Within a right balance of enjoying the present and not worrying about tomorrow (Matthew 6:34) it is important to envision your children about their future. Encourage them to believe that they can attempt anything they want if they believe in themselves and the value of their chosen path. Most importantly, teach them how to seek God's will about choices and decisions, and how to measure up their lifestyle against the word of God. Within the security of those guidelines, the world is indeed at their feet.

Encourage each other

As people

It is sometimes possible to feel that your own identity has been submerged in the demands, cares and emotions of parenthood. You are no longer just yourself, but someone's mother or father. You are viewed and perhaps even judged by others through your children. Most of your time and conversation seems to be concerned with children and related topics. This perhaps might apply particularly to the mother who has chosen to care full-time for her children, but it is also applicable to mothers and fathers in paid employment. There is a danger of being so child-centred in your approach that there is no space for yourselves as separate people and as a couple. Yet it is important to have that space, in order to develop as an individual and, para-doxically, to be a better parent. This is the argument that many parents make to justify an early return to paid employment, and there is much sense in it. However, with a bit of deter-mination and creativity, it should be possible to provide sufficient stimulation and external interest without necessarily returning to a paid job.

- Make a positive effort to talk with your spouse about things which have nothing to do with the home or the family. Try and keep your mind motivated and sharp with subjects completely unrelated to domesticity or your job. This could be current affairs, local issues, a hobby, fashion – anything which takes your interest and which is not to do with the children!

- Recognise that the need in you both for individual space is not a rejection of each other and make it possible for each partner to have time alone. For example, take up an evening class or a sport and have some time when you are away from the family. The logistics of giving each other regular 'time out' are not always easy, but it is worth the effort. Make sure that the division of time is fair, and don't begrudge it!

- Do a 'childcare swap' with a friend. If you are at home during the day, team up with someone in a similar situation and look after each other's children so that you can each have some time during the week. Use the time for yourself, not for the housework! (This never used to work very well for me, because I had too many children to do a fair swap!)

- Go away on your own for at least a night. Not every week, of course, but at least once a year. Leave your partner and/ or other trusted carers in charge, and get completely away, to friends, perhaps (as long as they have no children!) or even a bed and breakfast! It is so valuable to step back from the hurly-burly of everyday life, to relax and reflect. You return a renewed person, to discover that absence has made everyone's heart fonder. (At least, that's the theory, and it usually works!)

Making time for yourself and encouraging your partner to do so is not being selfish, opting out or neglecting your children. It is actually a means of growth and thus enhancement for you and the whole family. Time away from the demands of your everyday life can restore your depleted resources and renew your mental and physical energy. I used to go to a jazz dance class once a week, and though I never felt like going, and it was a real hassle to organise myself to get there, I always loved it when I finally got started, and felt so much better for it. Since we adopted Robert, I have returned to Romania several times for a long weekend, and know that these trips have helped me in my parenting. This is not just because I have been somewhere that has moved me and made me realise again how precious my family is, but also because the sheer joy of having no one to be responsible for but myself has given me a new lease of life!

I could not have gone jaunting off without Graham's encouragement and support. He has always respected and affirmed me as a person first and a mother second. That is quite important. There has never been any hint of the 'little woman at home' syndrome. The decision to make motherhood a full-time career was a joint one, and he has always helped to make it as fulfilling and enjoyable as possible. It is so important to encourage each other to maintain an individuality in life and faith even when the pressures of family life are at their greatest.

As parents

As has been mentioned several times, parenting is a vulnerable job, and couples need to encourage each other in it. Remember, encourage means 'to stimulate, motivate, animate, embolden, promote and cultivate; to impart courage, inspiration and resolution'! We need all of that as parents! I find far more value in a word of encouragement from Graham, who knows what life is really like for us, than from others who do not know the full story. (I still welcome encouraging words from anyone who cares to give them, though!)

We need to be praised in the things which are going well, and supported in the things which aren't. When I was at home full-time, with three children under four and another on the way, I needed to be told I was doing a good job. It was not enough to believe it for myself (which I didn't always, anyway!). I needed to have Graham's appreciation of what I was doing, just as he needed to be appreciated for all he did on top of a day's hard work in the office. It is much easier to see and remember the things which have gone wrong during the day than all the things which have gone right. Point out where your partner has handled a situation well or had significant input into one or other of the children and value him for it. There seems to be something in (fallen) human nature which makes it more instinctive to see a fault and criticise than to see a virtue and praise it, but the praise is far more important and helps to make us better parents.

Where we are struggling, it is imperative that our partner supports us in it and helps us to see the problem in perspective. Just because you are consistently finding one aspect of your child's behaviour difficult to handle, and keep making mistakes, does not mean that you are a failure as a parent, or that solutions will never be found. You need someone to tell you that and to help you, in a non-judgmental way, to find those solutions.

Finally, we need to encourage each other to enjoy being parents! Encouragement *is* sometimes needed, because it is easy to become weighed down with the responsibilities of family life, or the sheer number of chores waiting to be done (over-flowing laundry baskets, an ironing basket that requires a weightlifter to move it, the siren call of Sainsbury's . . . !) Get each other to 'lighten up' and be silly every now and again. Take time to hang around with the children and join in their activities instead of supervising while simultaneously doing two or three other things. Play practical jokes – not everyone's cup of tea, I know, but the children love it! By whatever means, draw each other into the wonder, joy and fun of parenthood.

9

Encouragement – A Two-Way Process

Therefore, encourage one another and build each other up,
just as in fact you are doing.
(1 Thessalonians 5:11)

Encouragement is not an optional extra, but an important function for every Christian. The Bible includes it in a list of important ministries, as can be seen from the above verse. Also, in 2 Timothy 4:2, Paul urges the reader to *'be prepared in season and out of season; correct, rebuke and encourage – with great patience and careful instruction'*. The previous chapter examined how significant this ministry is for ourselves as individuals and within the family. However, there is a much wider scope to the 'ministry of encouragement' than that, and I believe that God wants us to use what we have learnt in our own lives to help others.

Encourage others

In the church

Within our extended family of the church, there will be many parents experiencing the pressures and perplexities of bringing up children, who urgently need encouragement. If we are willing, God will give us opportunities to be a resource for them. Talk to other parents in the crèche or Sunday school or youth group, and share what you have been learning. I find personally that such lessons usually have their humorous side, and that the humour assists me in communicating the particular point under discussion. Little anecdotes about the family's misbehaviour or misunderstandings help you identify with the other parents, particularly if the laugh is against you! If you can be honest about your own struggles and achievements, you will be a source of great encouragement to others in a similar situation.

It is a fair assumption that you are not the only one who occasionally feels inadequate or guilty or totally drained. It is good if you can use your own experience to support others who are feeling the same. Often, they are reluctant to confess their emotions, but once you have admitted to similar ones yourself, then they are relieved to be able to talk about them. We have all had the experience of feeling so much better once we have 'got something off our chest'. Together, you can find solutions to the challenges facing you.

It is important to notice the positive characteristics of your friends' children and make sure you actually tell them! I have been so 'blessed' (and surprised, I have to say!) when people have made a point of coming to tell me about my child's good behaviour or mature conversation or kind act. There is always the temptation to belittle the compliment – and the child – by some deprecatory response such as, 'Well, that makes a change!' or 'Are you talking about my child?!' I think this comes out of a desire not to boast about one's children, and also, for some, a deep feeling of unworthiness as a parent. 'If they only knew what failures we have with this child, they wouldn't say such nice things,' goes the thinking. I have learnt to take a positive line now; 'Thank you for saying that. It's great to have the encouragement. Yes, he can be very kind and thoughtful at times. It's a lovely side of his character.' By accepting the encouragement and reiterating it myself, I am allowing the truth of it to enter my thinking.

God uses other people as a means of giving you his encouragement. Make sure that he can use you in that capacity as well. The most obnoxious child has some delightful characteristics, and it is worth making a point of discovering them and telling his parents about them.

Sometimes, though, encouragement takes the form of talking frankly about the weaker areas of someone else's parenting, of *'speaking the truth in love'* (Ephesians 4:15) in order to build them up. This is a more sensitive issue, as the last thing you want is to appear interfering or disapproving. The church is there to share problems as well as joys, and we cannot afford to have an attitude of 'it's not my business'. Some time ago, one of the children from a family who had recently joined the church consistently behaved disruptively in the children's meetings. The children's workers dealt with him as best they could, and maintained a loving and caring attitude towards him. But there came a point when, for the sake of the child as well as the rest of the children in the meeting, they felt that they needed to talk to the parents. It was felt that there were underlying problems which needed addressing, in a spirit of concern and commitment. At first, the parents were understandably defensive, but as they realised that people were 'on their side' rather than criticising, they opened up and shared the problems they were having with this child. With the encouragement and help of a few children's workers, they were able to see a great improvement in the situation.

There might be times when you feel moved to speak to another parent about vulnerable areas you have noticed in their family life. It is important first to examine your own motives before doing so, and approach it very much as someone who understands and is concerned, rather than one who points the finger in accusation. There needs to be an atmosphere of trust, so that everyone knows that any comments are given in an attitude of caring rather than judgment. It is not easy to be told that your little darling is behaving defiantly or rudely (even though you are all too aware of the fact yourself) and you need to be secure in the love of the person who is bringing up the subject. We all need to receive and give support and encouragement but it is essential that this is done in a loving, non-judgmental way.

Encouragement can include talking honestly about negative behaviour or feelings, but always with the aim of building the other person up. Your purpose is to reassure other parents that they are doing a good job as godly parents, not to join them in a downward spiral about the stresses and strains of family life! Even if a parent has a serious problem with their child, such as trouble at school or a teen suspected of trying drugs, there is still room for encouragement. Comments such as, 'Goodness, that *is* bad. You must feel *terrible*. What on earth are you going to do?' are not very helpful. Courage is needed, and support and some guidance. You may not have the experience to give guidance, but you can help them find the right advice and you can keep in touch with them during the crisis times, encouraging them to stick to the biblical principles of parenting throughout. The key is compassion. All that we do and say as we encourage others should be motivated by that. Not an inner, unacknowledged feeling of superiority, nor a sense of duty, but the love and compassion of God flowing out to those around us.

A good idea is to get together with other parents for Bible study and prayer. This does not necessarily have to be on the subject of parenting, but to encourage each other in your relationship with the Lord. Only other parents will completely understand the particular pressures of maintaining a vibrant walk with God amid the demands of family life. They are therefore the best people to help each other. Obviously, regular study and prayer times are difficult to keep up, but reasonably frequent get-togethers as the opportunity arises are a lifeline. As we allow the word of God to dwell in us richly (Colossians 3:16), we will be empowered to tackle our responsibilities with renewed vigour! Occasional Bible studies specifically on children and parenting are very valuable and inspiring, and probably more helpful done in a small group so that you can gain from other people's insights. There are quite a few studies on this subject on the market, or just using a concordance to do a word study can be immensely beneficial.

Prayer is a vital element in encouragement. You can pray generally for those parents you know, and also about specific situations or problems. Likewise, you can ask other people to pray for you. Some parents find it helpful to get together to pray, while for others it is more practical to reserve it for their private prayer time. I often pray for people when they come to mind during the day, and if I am aware of a particular issue I can bring it before the Lord frequently as I go about my other business. Do make sure, though, that if you say you will pray for someone you actually do. I confess that there have been times when I have told someone I would pray and then it has completely slipped my mind. Not at all good on my part, and I have felt very bad about it, but God has been faithful anyway! It is important to let the other person know that you have prayed, so that they are aware that they are being supported, and tell them any thoughts which came to you while you were praying. I have known instances where someone has been praying for me and has come to tell me of a verse or thought that came to them. They have not been able to make much sense of it, but it has been exactly what I needed to hear, God speaking specifically to me through another person.

Outside the church

Once you have children, you develop a whole new circle of friends and acquaintances, from people you went to ante-natal classes with, through those at toddler group, playgroup, to school and all the extra-curricular activities which ensue – ballet, swimming, gym club, football, music, Brownies, Scouts and so on. Wherever you take your children, there will be parents, and these parents, like you, need encouragement, a listening ear and support in the ordinariness as well as the crises of family life. Some of my closest friends are those I made when the children were small and we clung to each other in the 'same boat', desperately trying to keep it afloat at times!

It can be daunting when you are a young mum to venture into an already established group of parents, such as the toddler or playgroup, and the school playground can be positively frightening, with its small groups of parents who all seem to stare at you and stop talking just as you pass! However, if you take your courage in both hands and begin to make conversation, you will find that very soon you have made some friends of like mind. You can always ask about other people's children, or make complimentary comments about them. That is a guaranteed conversation starter! As you slowly become part of this new social grouping, you will discover increasing opportunities to encourage those around you.

Another good way to become more integrated into the community of parents is to join one of the many committees which exist to ensure the smooth operation of the various organisations linked to the children. Being a committee member also has the added advantage of giving you some influence over the way these organisations are run. In my time, I have been on the committee of the local under-fives group for a few years, the York branch of the Pre-school Playgroups Association (PPA), various 'Friends of the School' associations and PTAs. These have invariably been great fun, and have provided opportunity for friendships to develop as well as opinions and decisions to be voiced. Graham never used to believe that we did any work, since I came back from meetings regaled with wine, cake and amusing anecdotes!

When we were first in Poppleton, there was no playgroup, though there was an excellent nursery unit attached to the primary school. However, several of us felt that a playgroup would be a good transition from toddler group to nursery, and could offer an extra element to the under-fives in the village. It took a lot of research, phone calls and hard work, but eventually we achieved our aim and established a good playgroup, which is still flourishing eight years later. It was tremendously satisfying to have initiated such a venture and contributed something worthwhile to the whole community. And a side effect was that I got to know many people very well!

In a very natural way, because it is part of my life, I talk to my friends about the Lord and how important he is in our family life. Whether we feel like it or not, as Christians we do have an extra element in our parenting, a security that God is guiding us and the principles of his word to stick to. Our relationship with him will be expressed through how we are in our everyday lives, how we cope with crises, and our relationships with others. Often, there is no need to speak specifically of the Lord, but just to reach out with his love to those around us, to listen, to care or to help. Yet there are other times when there have been opportunities to talk about God. While in no way ever wanting to preach or imply that we have got it all right (which self-evidently is not the case!), I try to show that we have a resource in our parenting, and to share some of God's principles when appropriate.

Sometimes people just need to hear a word of praise or admiration, an affirmation that they are doing well in their parenting, and that their children are OK. At other times, there are specific problems that they are struggling with, and for which they are looking for answers. I can remember my friend

Anna coming to the house practically in tears. Her elder child was being bullied at school, to the point where he had run away during playtime, and she did not know how to deal with the situation, both emotionally and practically. I did not really have any answers myself, but I listened and comforted, and then made some suggestions based on the Bible. I did not have a 'holier than thou' attitude, nor was it a counselling session: just two friends sharing a problem together and seeking a solution in God's ways. And it worked! The child was able to talk through his problems and the situation improved from that time on.

I have prayed for and with friends and their children, and seen answers. It feels frightening and a bit risky to make the initial suggestion. What if they are offended, or deeply embarrassed? What if they reject me, and tell the whole playground about my weird beliefs and habits? Yet if you feel God telling you to pray for them, you have to offer! I'm sure that God wants our spiritual lives to be a very natural part of our everyday business, whether we are with Christians or not, so that praying for someone or mentioning the Lord is second nature and not a big, cringe-making deal on anyone's part.

A friend of mine had a baby who was discovered rather late to have congenital dislocation of the hips. Obviously, she was very upset, and panicking about the implications. I too was upset, imagining how I would feel in the same situation. As we sat and talked, and my friend cried, I felt very strongly that the Lord wanted me to pray for the little girl. She was a pathetic sight, her legs splayed out because of a splint across her pelvis, struggling to drag herself around. Eventually, the compulsion to pray for her overcame my natural reluctance and I asked if I might pray, explaining that I believed that God could help her. My friend agreed, and I prayed quietly and simply for her. Within months, the splint was off, and now, ten years later, she is a normal twelve-year-old, who has had no further trouble with her hips. Other children in similar situations go on to have many operations throughout their lives. Whether this was a miraculous intervention or something which happened within the course of nature is not important. God wanted to make it clear that he has the power of healing, however he chooses to use it, and though my friend is not yet a Christian, I know that she was touched by the Holy Spirit that day.

More often, I tell someone that I will pray about their situation, and do so at another time, always making sure that they know I have prayed. I am not 'religious' or patronising about it, but just allow prayer and the Lord to be mentioned in a very natural, low-key way as we are talking. My experience is that, on the whole, people appreciate being prayed for, even if they themselves do not believe. They also desire the certainty of faith in this world of uncertainties. If they do not have that conviction themselves, they are grateful to lean on yours in times of trouble. There have been many times when I have been chatting to someone by the school gate or as we waited in the windy playground for the nursery to come out, and discovered that the person is going through a really difficult time: a death in the family, perhaps, or a recent miscarriage or a child seriously misbehaving at school. In those circumstances, expressions of sympathy and concern are the essential response, but I often conclude by saying that I will pray for her. It is another means of showing that I care, and that God does too. As you encourage friends in the community, and exercise your faith in regard to them, you will find that things start to happen, both for them, and for yourself!

Occasionally, I even encourage complete strangers with children! This varies from the obligatory crooning over a new baby to sympathetic noises to the harassed mother of the screaming toddler in the supermarket queue. I have been there, and I know what it feels like to receive hostile glares as I struggle with the shopping and the recalcitrant child. One lady in the checkout next to me even put her fingers in her ears as Barnaby indulged in one of his more spectacular tantrums! (It wasn't long before I stopped taking children shopping altogether and only now have I recovered sufficiently to take one at a time to push the second trolley!) While people culturally are quite reluctant to speak to strangers, you never know what a passing encouraging word might do for them. If you see a parent in trouble with a child, try to help if it is appropriate. There is a subtle balance between interfering and walking by on the other side. Ask for God's wisdom, and then trust your instinct one way or another. There used to be in our society a much greater level of involvement in each other's lives. The norm nowadays is for people to maintain a self-sufficiency and independence from each other. However, I believe God wants there to be a restoration of mutual care, support and encouragement in the community.

Encouragement can take many practical forms. Swap useful books or magazines or send encouraging cards. Sometimes, on the spur of the moment, I might buy a friend a bunch of flowers if I know she needs cheering up a bit. Have people round for coffee, so that the children can play and the adults chat together. In his less sensitive moments, Graham used to tease me for the amount of time I appeared to spend drinking coffee with friends. My indignant response, suitably super-spiritual, was that I was about the Lord's work! It was doing us all good to get together occasionally, and therefore making us better parents. Anyone who has chosen to care full-time for their young children will recognise instantly the truth of this response! Another form of practical encouragement is to make a meal for someone if she is unwell, or offer to take the children away for a while to give her a break. The help is very welcome, but more so perhaps is the care and thoughtfulness which underpin it.

Be encouraged!

By the Lord

Believe that he is pleased with you, that he has called you to parent, and that he will not fail you (1 Corinthians 1:9). The Bible reverberates with God's pleasure in his people and his desire to provide us richly with '*everything for our enjoyment*' (1 Timothy 6:17). Therefore, he is not going to leave you to flounder in a task that is too difficult for you. By constantly (as opposed to occasionally, which anyone is allowed!) being discouraged, you are in reality questioning his ability to equip you for the task, and his faithfulness to complete the work he has begun. Are you '*confident of this, that he who began a good work in you will carry it on to completion*' (Philippians 1:6)? If not, ask God to give you that confidence, and ask his forgiveness for doubting him. As you pray, or just sit quietly before the Lord, relax and become aware of his joy in you. He will bring words and thoughts of encouragement in many ways, through the Bible, through songs, through other people. All you have to do is listen – and believe it!

My sister, on reading this paragraph, doubted that it could be that easy. She knows, she says, many mothers 'who just do not think that they are doing a good job, nor that they will ever do one'. I accept this, but can only reiterate that the Lord *can* change our thinking. Sometimes it is better to focus on our relationship with him, as the foundation for everything else, rather than the issues of parenting which seem to be causing the problem. As our relationship with the Lord deepens, so we will be encouraged and so our parenting will improve. It takes time and sometimes determination, but it does happen!

By your child

Your child's love for you, and her evident progress (however it might sometimes seem) is encouragement of itself. I sometimes look at our energetic, enormous children in wonder, hardly able to believe that I produced them. When you think how they have developed and all their achievements, it is bound to make you feel good! Take time to be encouraged by how your child is maturing, rather than dwelling on all the ways in which she is not.

Also, let her be a more direct encouragement. My children are always urging me on to do activities that I don't think I can do, like riding rollercoasters or writing a book! I have been very adventurous at times because of their enthusiastic encouragement. (They obviously haven't got to the age yet when to be seen with a mum doing slightly unconventional things is the height of embarrassment!) They are also good at telling me how capable and clever I am at various things. (No, I haven't brainwashed them, honest!) Even though one must discount childish exaggeration and lack of judgment, it is still very encouraging. To them, I am the best mum in the world, because I'm theirs, and that can be a very uplifting and restoring feeling. Wendy, one of my questionnaire respondents, wrote that, for her, the most rewarding aspect of parenting was being told by her children that they love her, being written letters and given hugs, just because she's their mum.

Enjoy the encouragement your children can give you just by making you laugh. One of my friends said that sometimes the children bring tears of laughter to her eyes. I'm sure that we can all identify with that! Another friend told me of how she had been watching a documentary with her daughter and the subject of illegitimate children arose. The interviewee spoke of her mother bringing disgrace to the family as she had been born out of wedlock. Louise questioned this 'wedlock business' and asked if she had disgraced the family as she had been born in

York and not Wedlock! We all have times when the children come out with priceless gems, and the enjoyment that they bring can be a great encouragement to us.

By other people

Just as you endeavour to encourage others, so also be encouraged by them. Accept compliments and praise from others without qualifying them with disclaimers about your short temper or useless baking! As it says in the Bible, *'pleasant words are a honeycomb, sweet to the soul and healing to the bones'* (Proverbs 16:24). And if someone does encourage you with a word which is not so pleasant, touching on the more vulnerable areas of your parenting, try to accept it in the spirit in which it is offered, secure in yourself and in the love of the other person.

By looking after yourself

You will feel more encouraged about yourself if you are in good health in body, mind and spirit. In the hurly-burly of caring for those who are dependent on you, it is easy to neglect yourself. Many parents (particularly mothers who stay at home to work full-time with their children) do not eat very well, and do not get enough proper exercise. You might feel that you are on the go all day, and constantly nibbling left-overs, so that by the end you are exhausted and full up. But exercise and diet of this kind is not really conducive to fitness and health. It is important to take time to eat and exercise healthily. A brisk walk or cycle ride might be all that is needed, or perhaps the discipline and fun (?) of an aerobics or dance class, or the refreshing of a weekly swim. It is worth trying to get into a routine with it, as then you are more likely to keep going.

The benefits of feeling and looking more fit are wide ranging, affecting energy levels, looks, general well-being and self-esteem. You will also feel more encouraged about life in general if you feel you look good. As I have considered full-time motherhood as much a career as teaching, I have tried to look 'professional' as much as possible. Of course, I frequently dress in jeans or the dreaded leggings, for comfort and practicality, but I also quite often wear skirts and dresses, and nearly always wear some make-up. It is what I would do if I were going out to work, and I want to maintain the same standards at home. It makes me feel better about myself and is also more attractive for Graham and the children. It is worth repeating that looking after yourself is not a selfish thing to do. On the contrary, the whole family will benefit!

Encouragement for fathers – by a father!

Just as men are not so naturally inclined to show emotion in their dealings with other people, neither does mutual encouragement come as easily to men as it does to women. In my experience, expressions of empathic interest or the words 'well done' are rarely seen or heard in a male-dominated environment. The man who makes it to the top or stands out in his achievements might receive a lot of accolades or rewards, but most people, by definition, are not included in this.

However, you only need to look at the lives of some of the great men in the Bible to realise that there is nothing 'wimpish' about giving or receiving encouragement. Paul began most of his letters to the churches with expressions of thankfulness for them. These were to churches made up of ordinary people, not 'super-saints', and in many cases the letter may have been to a church that was causing him a lot of concern. Joshua was able to lead the people of Israel through very difficult circumstances because of the coaching and confidence-building that Moses had given him. David was on many occasions overwhelmed by the enormity of the opposition he faced, but was given new determination and hope from men around him. The catalogue could continue.

There have been many occasions when I have been feeling low because I felt as if much of family life consisted of trying to minimise squabbles, or because our boys patently were not the model children I subconsciously and unrealistically would like them to be. Then sometimes out of the blue will come a statement from a friend or acquaintance concerning some positive attribute of one or more of the children, or how much they enjoy their company. All too often we lose our sense of perspective, and we therefore need each other's encouragement to help keep a balanced view, and a sense of worth in what we are doing as fathers.

I offer below a few hints as to how to both give and receive encouragement in our role as fathers.

- **Take an interest in other men's experiences and challenges as fathers**. Don't just ask other parents how their children are doing and comfortably hide behind safe topics such as schooling, but show that you are concerned about the parents' emotional well-being too.

- **Don't let negative talk from other fathers go unchallenged**. Many fathers I come across appear to focus almost entirely on the nuisance value of children, or appear to think it is funny to talk disparagingly about their children. (This is of course even worse if they belittle them while their children are there, as it does a lot to undermine their self-esteem, quite apart from creating an unhealthy role model for them.) A gently given counter-view or a pertinent question is often called for.

- **Let your own speech be positive**. It is easy to focus on all the difficulties but not the rewards of parenting. One of my favourite sayings to counter negative talk, which now sounds rather hackneyed but is nevertheless very true, is that there is nothing of real value in life that does not have some pain or cost involved. This very much applies to bringing up children. Yes, there is sacrifice involved, but the rewards are great.

- **Give family life its due worth in your conversations**. In the same way that some women who choose full-time motherhood in place of paid employment find that society does not attribute much worth to their vocation, men are not necessarily given recognition for aspiring to be effective fathers and making family life a high priority. We have a skewed system of values which openly rewards men who have done well in their careers while their private family life may have suffered through neglect.

- **Be real**. This is notwithstanding the need to let our conversations focus on what is good and upbuilding. One of the keys to giving or receiving encouragement is to be open and honest. Of course there is only a limited number of people with whom we can bare our soul. Nor am I suggesting that we should go out fishing for compliments, but it is important to be able to be real with each other, and not to gloss over our feelings or experiences. I am convinced that many men want and need to talk about the challenges they face as fathers, if only they can get through the barrier of thinking that such talk is a sign of weakness, or that parenting is just a subject of discussion for women.

- **Build yourself up in God**. Bring your needs as a father into your prayer life, and keep in mind that your role as a father is one which God has both called you to and equipped you for. This brings fresh courage and resolve in your dealings with your children.

* * *

Supporting, affirming, motivating others is a very positive activity which not only furthers the purposes of God in the world but also contributes greatly to our own well-being. As the Bible points out, *'he who refreshes others will himself be refreshed'* (Proverbs 11:25). The very act of encouraging someone else becomes encouragement for ourselves. We feel excited and fulfilled to be doing God's work, and our spirit is lifted accordingly. The positive words we say to others reverberate in our own lives and become reality when we need them. It might not be as high-profile as preaching or leading worship, but encouragement is as valid a ministry as any of them!

10

Adopted into the Family (Robert – 'Bright and Famous')

Theirs is the adoption as sons; theirs the divine glory, the covenants, the receiving of the law, the temple worship and the promises.
(Romans 9:4)

Robert is the only one of our children whom we did not name ourselves, because he already had a name when we first met him, in a damp, rusting cot in a Romanian hospital. Although we would not have necessarily chosen that particular name ourselves, its meaning does express some of his character. He is indeed quite famous, although we did not particularly choose for him to be so. It just happened! As an individual, he is widely known locally, where people took him to their hearts both before and after the adoption. He came to symbolise the struggle against neglect and hardship which moved so many people. Now, his story in published form (*Romanian Rescue*, Hodder and Stoughton, 1997) means that he is known to a greater number of people. Robert's personality, too, is the type which ensures that he stays in the memory! He is not the sort of child who merges into the background! He is very friendly and chatty to anyone who comes within his range, and he usually assumes that everyone is there for his pleasure and entertainment.

He is also famous as a Romanian orphan. The plight of those children was headline news for some time, and everyone was shocked by the appalling images on their television screens. Because Romania was within reach, unlike some other troubled places in the world, people filled vans with aid and set off to help. The whole issue of Romania was in the public con-sciousness for a long time, and very many gave a great deal to assist. Even now, occasionally, there are follow-up stories which highlight the situation. As one of the children who escaped from the hardship of the orphanage, he was bound to hold some interest for those who knew his background.

The miracle is that the other element of Robert's name also holds true for him. Despite the label of handicap, and the appalling deprivation that he suffered, he is indeed a bright, lively, cheerful child, a shining example of the Lord's saving power. In the early days, the light in his eyes was dimmed, submerged by misery and fear, but now they shine with all the pleasures and excitement of childhood.

All adopted children are, in their own way, bright and famous, if only to their adoptive parents. They are singled out, celebrated especially, and their coming brings a special brilliance and delight into their new homes. In many ways, parenting the adopted child is no different to parenting a birth child, and in other ways it is very different, bringing its own special joys, challenges and rewards. Every adoption, like every birth, is unique, and some of the things which we have experienced and learnt might not apply to other adoptive parents. For instance, I believe that there is a distinction in experience between those who have no natural children when they adopt, and those who have. I will not have undergone some of the pressures which couples with no natural children have suffered, and likewise they will not be able to identify with some of the stresses I have felt as both a birth and an adoptive mother.

This chapter serves as an acknowledgment that any book on

parenting needs to consider the particular demands and enjoyment of being an adoptive parent. There are other books which deal with the subject in more depth than can necessarily be addressed here, and some of these are listed under 'Useful Resources'.

Adoption – a scriptural perspective

Adoption is not an inferior alternative; it is a second and equally valid chance of life. Numerous couples turn to adoption when all else has failed. They have exhausted the possibilities of fertility treatment, their finances and themselves. So they choose adoption as a last resort. This is an understandable course of action, and I have great compassion for those who suffer the grief of childlessness. Many come to terms with it in a very positive way, yet there are others who miss something wonderful because they see adoption as 'second best', a buttress to their failure as biological parents. Unfortunately, many other people not directly involved in adoption see it in that way as well, perpetuating a wrong attitude to the whole process. Not so long ago, adoption was stigmatised. Parents tried to keep it quiet that they had adopted a child, and children were ashamed to admit that they were adopted, if indeed they were even told the fact.

Yet adoption was in the heart of God from the beginning, and he actually equates it with new birth. The Bible uses the image of adoption to describe the new, second birth that we have when we become Christians. In Ephesians 1:5, we are told that *'in love, he predestined us to be adopted as his sons through Jesus Christ, in accordance with his pleasure and will'*, and in Romans 8:23, the writer pictures us waiting *'eagerly for our adoption as sons'*. The textual note to this verse in the NIV Study Bible comments: 'Adoption was common among the Greeks and Romans, who granted the adopted son all the privileges of a natural son, including inheritance rights. Christians are adopted sons by grace; Christ, however, is God's son by nature.'

As Christians, we are all adopted children, given the rights and privileges of birth children. The Lord sees adoption as a means of rebirth into his family. Therefore, we must never see the means by which we obtained this child as any less 'natural' than the biological method by which most children enter their family. Instead, view the adopted child as having new birth into the family, as valid a member as any other. A great many people ask me about Robert's 'real' parents, to which I reply that Graham and I are! The legal act of adopting him made us his *only* parents and cut him off from his past.

This is a picture of what the Lord does for us when we become Christians. Of course, we still want Robert to know about his origins and to be proud of his heritage, but he is free of any ties to his past. When we returned to Romania in 1997, and he looked at the place where he had spent so much of his time, it was as a completely different person. He could not really identify himself as the little boy who had spent so many miserable years in a cot. That is how we should be as Christians, aware of where we came from, still having contact with people, places and situations from our past, but no longer tied to them or ruled by them.

At adoption, Robert also became a British citizen, taking on the citizenship of his parents, with all the rights and responsibilities of one born in this country. This also is an image of the Christian. Our new status as sons and heirs of God gives us a different citizenship – '*many live as enemies of the cross of Christ. Their destiny is destruction, their god is their stomach, and their glory is in their shame. Their mind is on earthly things. But our citizenship is in heaven*' (Philippians 3:19–20). So we live according to different laws and are subject to a higher authority, bestowed on us at our adoption.

Adoption – an emotional maelstrom

The actual process of adopting a child, whether from this country or abroad, is extremely stressful. There is the pressure of the Home Study, and the strain of wondering whether you are 'good enough' to be parents. I have often thought that if natural parents were required to undergo the rigorous scrutiny of absolutely every aspect of their lives that adoptive parents are, and then be examined at the end of it and passed or failed for parenthood, the population would decrease dramatically! Our Home Study was conducted by a very sympathetic social worker, but it took months and we did feel very much as if we were on trial.

Then, there is always uncertainty about when or whether the child will materialise. Often, after waiting months or even years, adoptive parents have only a few days to prepare themselves for this most life-changing of events. This can be quite a shock! One does not have the slow realisation and months of making ready afforded by pregnancy. Because the child is not of your genes, there is the underlying worry, often voiced by insensitive friends or relatives, that he'll 'turn out badly' or have some dreadful inherited disease or that you won't understand or like his character. These are worries and fears, perhaps seldom expressed, which many adoptive parents feel, and often they come on top of years of striving to conceive, and all the attendant stress and grief of infertility or miscarriage.

It is as well to acknowledge the emotions of adoption and try to deal with them by allowing them expression. Otherwise, they can shake the very foundations of your parenting of this needy child. As Christians, we can feel guilty if we have negative feelings about something which God has ordained and brought about. I remember realising, after Robert had been with us for some months and I had been very ill with hepatitis, that I felt quite resentful towards him because of all the problems and difficulties that had ensued as a consequence of adopting him. The last few weeks in Romania, desperately trying to complete the adoption there, the distress of constant visits to the orphanage, the tension, right up to the very end, of not knowing whether we would succeed – none of these emotions had been properly talked or worked through before I fell ill and then another set overlaid them.

I was horrified at myself when I realised how I was feeling towards Robert. After all, it was not his fault that I was weak and exhausted from illness, nor was he to blame for his persistent attention-seeking. My intellect acknowledged all of this, and my will continued to love him. But in my emotions I was angry and resentful at the price he had exacted from me and the family, and I became quite irritable and impatient with him.

I could not talk about this to anyone. Everyone was so proud of what we had done, and thought we were such good parents. How could I admit that, after all that we had been through to get him and all that he had been through in his young life, I was feeling negative towards him? I could not even really talk to Graham about it, because he was having enough trouble just holding the family together without the added burden of my emotional problems. In my weak state, I could not get anything into perspective, and struggled for some time before the obvious answer was the only way to go. I poured out my feelings to the Lord, knowing that he loves me anyway, and asked forgiveness for wrong attitudes and help and strength to continue in the path he had shown us. The release was gradual but wonderful. The situation improved from that time onwards, although there have been many instances since when I have had to repeat the process for one reason or another.

Adoption is as demanding and emotional a time as pregnancy and birth, if not more so, and we should not feel inadequate or a failure if sometimes those emotions threaten to overwhelm us. The Lord understands; he too has been through the longing and the hope, and even though he has not felt wrong feelings towards those he has adopted, he nonetheless has compassion on those of us who sometimes do. He *will* forgive, and he *will* help us to succeed. Often other people are a means of help, and it is valuable to be in contact with a support network who will be able to empathise and give helpful hints.

The British Association for Adoption and Fostering (BAAF) can put people in touch with others in their locality, and often there are other self-help groups available. The Citizens' Advice Bureau is a useful source of information. We have maintained contact with other people who have adopted from Romania, and also belong to an organisation called the Parental Network for Post-Institutionalised Children. We have found it immensely helpful to talk and share insights with others in a similar situation to ourselves. For other adoptive parents, follow-up assistance from a social worker or backing from a Christian counsellor have proved beneficial. Do whatever is most appropriate for your situation and personality, but do seek some kind of support. It is no admission of inadequacy, but an acknowledgment that adoption is a stressful experience which takes its toll. With some sympathetic, creative help, the emotions you have undergone can be transfigured to enhance and enrich your parenting skills.

A different kind of love

No one ever told me that the love would be different. I went on training courses, I read books, and helpful though they all were, no one mentioned that the love is different. Not inferior, not worse, but distinct. I do not feel the same about Robert as I do about the other children. I love them all equally but in different ways. Barnaby asked me the other week (for no apparent reason!) whether I loved Daddy more than I loved them, and I paused before answering. The love I have for Graham is not 'more' or 'deeper' or 'better'. It is a different kind of love;

impossible to quantify such depth and quality of feelings. So it is with Robert; he brings out a whole different aspect of my maternal feelings. I don't have an innate understanding of him as I do of the others, because he does not have my genes within him. I can't identify with him in quite the same way. Yet I have felt more intense emotions for him than for any other of my children. We are passionately bonded, even though I probably lose patience with him more frequently than the others. My covenant love for him has been tested and proved. There is no question of favouritism or loving one less than another, but perhaps of instinctive as opposed to learned love. They are both valid and equal, and there should be no guilt about the difference.

Family adjustments

This applies more to families where there are already siblings. Unless your adopted child is a very young baby, which is increasingly rare in these days when abortion and lone parenting are both socially acceptable, then more adjustments need to be made than if a birth child was entering the family. The adopted child might have some behavioural difficulties because of his background. He may be withdrawn or very easily upset, or aggressive. He might not want to play or he might insist on running every game. He may try to run away, or he may scream and shout, or defecate behind the sofa. Whereas with a new baby there is time for brothers and sisters to adjust, since the baby does not do much more than cry, eat and sleep, the adopted child intrudes into their everyday life in a much more dramatic fashion. He may be very close in age to another child, or he may disturb the 'pecking order' by coming in between two children previously next to each other in age. Suddenly, there is a complete stranger wanting to play with your toys and claim your Mummy as his own. It is not an easy adjustment to make. Home isn't comfortable or secure any more, and this isn't just a temporary arrangement; it's forever.

Usually, however, there is some time beforehand to prepare your other children for their new brother or sister, although it is necessary to be realistic and realise that the practice will probably be very different from the theory. We involved our children from an early stage in Robert's adoption. After some subtle idea planting, it became their suggestion to adopt him, and while we did not refer constantly to the adoption during the year it took to complete, there were many times when we prayed for Robert and for an end to the deadlock we were in. When I rang up to tell them that we had finally achieved our dream and rescued him from the orphanage, they were jubilant, running around wildly cheering.

Naturally, they had no idea what it would mean to have this little boy to be their brother, but the idea was so much part of their consciousness that by the time he arrived it felt quite normal for him to be there. At first, it was like having a one-year-old in the house, so that was quite easy to cope with, from their point of view. The boys enjoyed showing and teaching him things, and took personal satisfaction in his rapid progress. Now, he is completely integrated and treated no differently from the other brothers. There are aggravations and squabbles, of course, and sometimes they are really embarrassed by his inappropriate behaviour, but there is also laughter, teasing and fun.

The wider family

'He'll never be a grandchild of mine' were my father's words when we discussed with him our desire to adopt Robert. His response, though perhaps more extreme than some, typifies the wider family's reaction to adoption when it affects them personally. Some relatives do not like the thought of 'someone else's child' coming into the family. Others will have horror stories of adopted children who 'turned against' their adoptive families and perpetrated all sorts of dreadful deeds. It is very hard to contend against such opposition, particularly as you are likely to be very vulnerable emotionally at that point.

I was especially upset by predictions that our other children would suffer because of our adoption of Robert. I remember going to bed and crying about it all, shaken in my belief that we were doing the right thing in adopting him. I am not usually an adherent of the 'pick a verse, any verse' school of Bible study, but that night I felt a strong urge to look at the book of Isaiah. As I leafed through it, some verses leapt out of the page at me, and my spirit leapt as I read them:

> *All your sons will be taught by the LORD,*
> *and great will be your children's peace.*
> *In righteousness you will be established;*
> *Tyranny will be far from you;*
> *you will have nothing to fear . . .*
> *If anyone does attack you, it will not be my doing . . .*
> *no weapon forged against you will prevail,*
> *and you will refute every tongue that accuses you.*
> Isaiah 54:13–17

Of course, there is always a danger in taking Scripture out of context, but I firmly believe that God spoke to me through those words in Isaiah. In the five years since we adopted Robert, they have held true, and will continue to do so.

Try not to be too defensive if relatives react negatively to the idea of adoption. They too need time to adjust to the idea and cope with their own emotions over the issue. Believe that God has called you to this course of action, and don't be shaken from that. It is sad if others whom you love do not seem able to share your joy, but be patient; they will probably change their minds. My father has become much more mellow towards the idea, and takes quite an interest in Robert after all!

Developing an identity

The young man walked to the front of the church and, looking a little pale, began to speak. 'I'm so glad that I have God as my Father,' he said, 'because this week I discovered that my parents are not really who I thought they were. I am adopted, and I never knew. If I didn't know God's Father-love, I would feel even more devastated than I do now.' He was twenty-one and felt as if the bottom had fallen out of his world. Suddenly there was a whole group of people who were connected to him, whom he knew nothing about. He had a completely different history to the one he thought he had. The shock of discovery affected him deeply for a very long time.

We know of a couple in Romania who adopted a little girl (an unusual action out there, where there is still a stigma attached to adoption) and have steadfastly refused to tell her the truth about her birth. Even when she asked directly if she was adopted, having been told something by friends, they lied and told her that she was their natural child. What will such deception do to their relationship and her sense of self when she eventually finds out, as she inevitably will do?

Adopted children are understandably often confused about their identity. They have two sets of parents, and two starts in life. Were they a mistake the first time? Why didn't the birth mother keep them? Are they really a part of the family, or are they on the outside? What characteristics have they inherited from the birth parents? All these questions plague the child as he grows up, and gradually become more compelling as he struggles to discover who he really is. Robert has already asked, 'Why didn't Emilia [his birth mother] want me any more? Why did she leave me in the hospital?' Impossible questions to answer, but we do our best to explain that we do not really know why; perhaps it was because she was very poor, and couldn't manage to look after him. He hasn't yet begun to ask questions about his birth father, for whom we do not even have a name, but no doubt he will one day.

It is important that your child always knows that he is adopted, and that he is special. His background, however appalling it is, is part of him, his history, and therefore cannot be denied or ignored. If adopted children grow up knowing that they come from a different place but that now they have been chosen to live in and be part of this particular family, then they can be secure in that. There will be no hidden shocks for them; they have assimilated their past from an early age and can learn to be comfortable with it.

Always be ready to answer as fully as you are able any questions the child may have about his background and birth parents. These days, much is being made of 'open adoptions', where contact is maintained between the child and his birth parent or parents. It is perhaps premature to comment on how successful this method is, as it is still in the comparatively early stages of experimentation. My own personal opinion is that it might be too confusing and unsettling for all concerned, especially the child. Surely it is more difficult for the child to be assured of his place in the family if he is constantly being torn by seeing members of another family, to which, in a way, he also belongs? As has already been mentioned, adoption is a new start, a new life, and though it is important for the child to know about his past, that past should no longer impinge on a secure present.

However, that said, many teenagers, in the midst of coming to terms with themselves anyway, have a burning desire to seek their roots and discover their birth family. This can be hurtful to the adoptive parents, as if, after all they have done, they are being rejected. But this is not the case, just as it is not the case that natural parents are being rejected when their teens experiment with alternative lifestyles. Emerging adults are discovering that they are distinct from their parents, and that it is conceivable for them to have opposing ideas. Realisation dawns that they don't have to do what their family has always done and that there are very different ways of living. All life's possibilities are arrayed before them. They are testing various ideas and styles to see what suits them. Much of the time they feel moody and discouraged for no particular reason. Self-esteem sinks and feelings of inadequacy are covered up by arrogance and even aggression. For adopted children, this is the time when doubts and questions about their origins and value surface and cause heartache.

It is best, if possible, to remain understanding and loving, interested in what your child is feeling. Express your care for him at every opportunity. He needs to know more about the circumstances of his birth and what his birth parents were like, in an effort to know himself, but this is not a rejection of you as his real parents. If we can be as secure in our child's love for us as we want him to be in ours, then we will be able to deal better with the inevitable emotions surrounding any search and discovery of birth parents.

Robert expressed an interest in meeting Emilia when we were in Romania this summer, and we considered it very carefully. He was not very sure why he wanted to see her, but we respected his wishes and would have begun a search for her, except that several of our Romanian friends warned that it would not be very wise to do so. Apparently, she had married and had two further children (making six in all, including Robert) and it was thought that her husband did not know of Robert's existence. It could disrupt their lives forever if we turned up out of the blue. Moreover, our friends feared that they might turn nasty and demand money and that the situation would create a very upsetting memory for Robert and the other children. We bowed to their superior knowledge and explained as best we could to Robert. At eight years old, he was not too bothered. Perhaps in ten years' time he will try again, and we would not try to dissuade him, although there is potential for much trauma in such a meeting, were it to take place.

Our main role in helping him to discover his identity is to give him the security of unconditional love and as much information and explanation as we can. We have photographs, magazine articles and videos ready for when he wants to learn more of the general background to his adoption. My book, *Romanian Rescue*, as well as our friendships and journeys in Romania and all our memories, will create a personal resource for Robert to develop a sense of self-knowledge and pride in his history.

As the young student said in church, it is good to have God as Father. That is the best means of developing an identity. No matter what has happened before, your child can know the peace and security of having God as his Father. Encourage him to relate to the Lord in this way, and emphasise again and again how important he is to God and to you. This will build a confidence and stability into him which will not be overturned by the hurts and uncertainties arising from the past. The ultimate identity he can have is to be identified with the Christ who came to save him.

Just as one does not look at birth children and think back constantly to the pregnancy and labour which produced them, so one should not dwell unduly on the fact that a child is adopted. It is a fact, yes, but not one that should figure largely in everyday existence. Our concerns are for the present and the future rather than the past. Life goes on, and most of the time we forget that he is not 'flesh of our flesh'. Yet, undeniably there are instances or phases when we are forcibly reminded that this child has an extra history. At those times, draw on your own security in God, and hold on to the fact that this specific child was a gift from him. And ask for that extra power which is sometimes needed to parent the adopted child!

11

Special Parenting

It will be a special gift to them . . . a most holy portion.
(Ezekiel 48:12)

'*Handicapat*,' the nurse said, tapping her head and gesturing at the silent child in the cot, '*Este handicapat.*' With these words, we were entering a new realm as parents, one that we knew little about and which scared us. How would we manage with a child diagnosed as 'handicapped'?

There are many books – though few Christian ones – written on the subject of children with special needs, full of specialist advice and well-researched information. I do not pretend to write at such a level; it would be presumptuous of me to do so, as I can only approach the subject as a parent. But to attempt a book on parenting and exclude this important minority of children would be more presumptuous still.

When we first saw Robert, he certainly did not appear to be at a 'normal' stage in his development. He gazed vacantly into space, tapping his head every few seconds, and barely responded to anyone around him. He could not walk, talk or chew and was incontinent. This was to be expected, to some extent, in view of the appalling neglect and deprivation he had suffered. However, we could not discount entirely the possibility that there was something seriously wrong with him, and that he would never progress much further from the

177

unresponsive, uncomprehending child of that time. Since then, he has proved the Romanian authorities wrong and has progressed by leaps and bounds. Yet he is still classed as having 'learning difficulties' and is in the 'statementing system' at school. Academically, he is a few years behind his chronological age, and socially and behaviourally he is not age-appropriate at all. Now this could still be attributable to the developmental delay at the beginning of his life, and he may yet catch up completely. On the other hand, he might not. Meanwhile, he is in the 'special needs' category, (though I think that all children have their own special needs!) and not always that easy to live with.

Parenting a child with special needs is one of the most demanding areas of parenthood, but can also be one of the most rewarding. I am always overwhelmed with admiration and humility when I meet parents with children who have severe disabilities. These parents have given up their lives for their children in a way not experienced by the rest of us. We think that we have sacrificed a lot for our children, but it is nothing in comparison to those who care full-time or even part-time for children who cannot walk or talk or feed or clean themselves. Children in severe pain, children whose quality of life has been seriously limited, children who are dying. These parents have a capacity for selflessness and patience which perhaps they themselves did not realise they possessed. Yet they can also suffer all the emotions of parenthood more intensely – frustration, guilt, anger, hope, joy, despair – and need commensurately more support and understanding.

Christian parents also have other agonies to deal with as they come to terms with the fact that their baby has problems, that he will not be 'normal'. Is God's gift to them flawed? Or did he intend their beautiful child to be like this? In which case should they pray for healing, or accept that 'the Lord gives, the Lord takes away', and try to rejoice? Some parents even wonder if some punishment is involved, thinking that they have sinned and so brought on themselves this grief of a child who will struggle with everyday life. It is easy for the rest of us to fall into the trap of answering the complexity of these thoughts with a glib response. It is possible to show more sensitivity and try to emphasise the all-loving nature of God and his mercy, but ultimately we cannot understand the turmoil of thought and emotion which goes on in the hearts of parents faced with what seems like tragedy. But the Lord does understand, and he, always compassionate, will meet these parents in a very special way, giving them a strength and peace beyond their natural resources.

Out of my own experience and the limited research I have done into the subject, I have observed some general principles which have helped us in the parenting of our special child.

Understanding why a child behaves in a certain way does not necessarily make that behaviour any easier to deal with

Sometimes, if a friend observes Robert's behaviour or I describe it, the response is, 'Well, you can understand why he's like that, can't you, poor little thing.' This is undeniably true, and we, more than anyone, do have insight into the causes of his behaviour. We saw where he came from, and the appalling treatment and neglect he suffered, and so we know that the way he behaves is the logical outcome of the deprivation of his early life. Likewise, other parents of children with special needs usually have a very clear knowledge of the reasons underlying their child's behaviour and attitudes. They know, better than all others, the circumstances through which the child has to struggle and which affect him so deeply. They can usually understand perfectly why their child behaves as he does.

However, they still have to deal with that behaviour. It cannot be ignored, for it often has a detrimental effect on others around him, and also, in the long term, will have a detrimental effect on him. We have found that understanding *why* he is as he is does not actually help in handling him. That is a separate issue. We can say to ourselves, to the other children, to his teachers, 'Don't forget what a bad start he had,' or 'He has got a lot to put up with,' but we still have a responsibility to address the consequences of that bad start or those difficult circumstances. And we will still sometimes be made angry, frustrated, upset and exhausted by the behaviour patterns of the special needs child. This of itself is not a failure on our part; as in other areas of parenting, it is important that we can acknowledge those feelings without guilt or inadequacy. The challenge comes in how we handle such feelings.

Special in some ways but not in others

It is easy to make allowances for special needs children, because of the struggles they have. Your compassion for their problems can make your expectations different to those you would have for a 'normal' child. Obviously, you know your own child and what he is capable of, but it is sometimes *not* the kindest policy to allow him to 'get away with things' just because he has disabilities. Although of course the child will require different treatment in some areas, in others he should be treated exactly the same as any other child. You might feel it is cruel to discipline a child, for instance, for being rude or throwing things, because you know how frustrated he becomes with the limitations on his mind or body, but actually that child needs boundaries set, needs to know that you care enough to stop him, and that he is not so freakish as to be ignored when anyone else would be told off in the same situation. Like anyone else, they will test the boundaries to see how much they can get away with, but the reality is that they desperately need the security of those boundaries.

Bette M. Ross, in her book *Our Special Child* (Nelson Word Ltd, 1994), reports the reaction of her other children when asked, in adulthood, whether having a brother with Down's Syndrome had been detrimental to their own lives.

They insist not. 'It would have been different,' Jim said, 'if you had given Mike special treatment, you know, so that he was a spoiled brat or something.' 'I never felt he was "special". He was my brother, just like Jim. We used to fight with him as much as with each other,' Laurie added. 'You always made him do Saturday chores right along with the rest of us.'

We know some people who have adopted a severely disabled child from Romania. She is nine years old and barely able to walk. As little as a few months ago, she could only crawl. Now, she can totter about, but mostly has to be led because she cannot see very well, and might have an accident. She makes moaning noises and rocks her head at frequent intervals, but she cannot talk. She can communicate by touch, but often it is impossible to discover what she wants or what she is feeling. Since she came to live with them, about a year ago, the family have not had one night's uninterrupted sleep. Most nights they are woken three or four times by her cries and screams.

What impressed me most when I met the family was how 'normally' this little girl was treated, particularly by her parents. She was made to sit to the table for her meal, and was told off for messing about with her food, even though, much of the time, she had to be spoon fed. When she was offered something, she was required to respond, rather than having it put in front of her. Her parents and sister spoke to her constantly and expected answers, even if they were only grunts or nods. If she walked into something or refused to do what she was told, they got cross with her, as if she was a 'normal' child. This might seem unreasonable, but I firmly believe that their approach was helping the girl to progress. She was learning all the time what was appropriate, desirable behaviour, among people who loved her and had no doubt that she could achieve all that was expected of her. If they made allowances and did everything for her, then she would remain in the dreadful state in which they first met her. Obviously, she does have physical and mental limitations, but these are being minimised by the family's determination to treat her as normally as possible in areas where they might be tempted to give in to her.

The same applies to attainments. Our instinct is to protect our 'special' children from failure or harm, but it might sometimes be better to treat them as no different and encourage them to have a go at anything that takes their interest. Robert, for example, has joined in the class obsession with football. He really wanted to participate in the lunchtime matches, and insisted on taking his kit every day. We didn't feel totally happy about this, because we feared that he would be hurt by the experience. He is very unco-ordinated, and he also finds it very difficult to work in a team. He doesn't know the rules of football, but that doesn't stop him from trying to run the game. We knew that none of these qualifications would make him popular with the other players, all of whom seemed very competitive and perfectionist in their attitudes. Yet we could not deny him the chance to play just because we knew it would probably end in tears. We could only trust that he would learn quickly and that his peers would be tolerant. Neither hope has proved true yet, but we admire Robert's pluck in keeping going, and are pleased that he seems to enjoy the game despite the often cruel jibes of his 'friends' when he plays.

The urge to be the same as his peers is as strong in the special needs child as it is in any other, and it is important to make space for this if at all possible. We cannot stop them doing something because we fear failure. Doing the same as friends, whatever the trend of the moment might be, and being able to talk about it is often more meaningful than whether they are good at it. Parents are understandably protective, and sometimes the child just cannot join in. But there are other times when we have to let go and take the risk of hurt, in order for the child to identify himself with his peer group. And sometimes the child surprises everyone with what he can achieve with a bit of encouragement and effort!

Extra self-esteem needed!

As has been noted elsewhere, all children are vulnerable to low self-esteem, and can be devastated by criticism or teasing from adults or peers. Wrong or careless attitudes towards them can affect their thinking in adulthood and seriously impair their quality of life. This is especially the case with children who have physical or learning difficulties. They are usually only too aware of how different they are from their friends or from those they see in the street or on the television. Other children can be very cruel and use the physical or mental differences as a basis for teasing or even bullying. This inevitably leads to much heartbreak for child and parents, causing sadness or anger, according to the personality of the child, and a real undermining of self-confidence. Robert notices that his writing and reading are not as good as most of the others in the class, and that no one really wants to play with him at playtime. He usually shrugs this off, because he is a naturally cheerful child, but sometimes he is affected by the situation and becomes tearful. Other children in similar or worse situations find their inability to be the same as their peers very hard to handle. They can become withdrawn or aggressive or very timid and diffident.

It is hard for parents to know how to tackle this, beyond comforting the child at the time, expressing once again that unconditional love, and praising him for who he is and what he does achieve. We need to take every opportunity to build up confidence and self-esteem by affirming, praising and enabling him to shine in one sphere or another. If there is something in which he is particularly interested, then help him to participate in it. Find books and magazines about it, write to organisations connected with it, discover ways in which he can be involved.

Jenny, for example, was fascinated by dance. She had slight cerebral palsy and would never be able to master the more advanced steps or perform professionally, but she knew lots about dance and loved listening to the music and joining in the simpler routines. She watched the various classes with avid interest and used to invent new dances for them in her head. When her teacher discovered this, she encouraged Jenny to choreograph small pieces and found that she had a real talent for it. So Jenny found a valuable, creative part that she could do within her beloved dance and grew in self-confidence and fulfilment.

William loved wildlife. He was wheelchair bound, and had some learning difficulties as well, but his face lit up at the sight of animals and he would spend ages looking at books about them. His parents built on this interest, getting him a pet hamster and taking him to wildlife parks and zoos when they could. They got information from the World Wide Fund for Nature, and joined one of their 'Adopt an Animal' schemes. Gradually, William amassed quite a knowledge on the subject of animals, and his absorbing interest gave him a pleasure and confidence that he would not have achieved otherwise.

If it is at all possible, encourage a passion in your child, such as a hobby, an academic subject, a game, the computer or a musical instrument, because such a passion will go a long way towards compensating for the suffering these children have to undergo. They can become experts in their field, which will earn them respect from their peers and bolster their self-confidence immeasurably.

Special parents too!

Parenting a child with special needs means that you are a parent with special needs. It is important to be aware of the extra stresses on the family and to try and take account of that in your lifestyle. One of the hardest adjustments parents have to make is to come to terms with the fact that life is going to be very different to the way they thought and dreamed. Many hopes and plans will have to be laid aside as the reality of your child's disabilities hits home. It can be a distressing and painful time, but once that adjustment has been made the positives and compensations of the situation begin to assert themselves. The worst course to take is to carry on as if nothing was different, and try to live life as before. It is essential to acknowledge that you have needs too, brought on by this special child in your family, and to make room for those needs in your lives. Some tips which parents in such situations have passed on are:

- **Make space for yourselves**. Try to have some time on a regular and frequent basis away from the child. Perhaps your health visitor or GP could arrange respite care occasionally. There are organisations which link families up with other families who take the child out occasionally or have him to stay for a day or two. There are respite centres for more severely disabled or sick children. On a more informal basis, see if someone in the church who has a special interest in your child would be willing to care for him occasionally so that you can have a break. The release from responsibility and the need to be endlessly patient will do you all good!

- **Invest in your marriage**. Do all you can to maintain your physical, mental and spiritual oneness. This theme has been covered in Chapter 4, but it is worth repeating here, because the stresses of a child with disabilities can bring distance into a relationship. You both become so immersed in the practicalities and the sheer demands of caring for your child that your own relationship slips into the background. Many of the tensions about the child are transferred on to each other and never resolved properly. A communication barrier creeps up, and almost without realising it you have lost the closeness and friendship that you once had. Be aware that this is a danger, and resolve to prevent it by making each other top priority; not an easy feat, but worth the effort.

- **Encourage other people to have input into the child**. Often parents feel overprotective about their special needs child, and are reluctant to allow others to share the care. There is a feeling that it is too much trouble for someone else, or that no one understands the child as we do. I am, I have to admit, sometimes embarrassed by Robert's behaviour and don't want it exposed to others. Yet there is great benefit in letting other trusted people participate in the upbringing of your child. They will have fresh insight and fresh energy levels! You will be able to talk over concerns and triumphs with them. And it will make the child feel important to know that there is someone specially for him. Pray for a person or people who will have this function in your family, and then actively look for them!

- **Keep in contact with others in the same situation**. You are not alone in your circumstances, though it may often feel like it. Maybe there is someone in your area in a similar situation that you could get together with. The local grapevine is often good at giving this sort of information, and you might find much mutual help from meeting up occasionally. Alternatively (or perhaps additionally), there is a support group or parent network for almost every disability and illness and these are worth joining. Self-help groups can give empathy and fellowship in a stressful situation, as well as good practical advice. Sometimes they have information about new research into your child's illness, or new treatment not widely available. The organisation can form a pressure group for change in law or policy when necessary, and can reduce that dreadful feeling of powerlessness and dependency which can overwhelm at times.

- **Enlist the help of professionals whenever possible**. Although they can sometimes be intimidating and give conflicting advice, they do have resources at their disposal which can aid the progress of your child. And they have an expert knowledge of your child's condition which is vital. They are there to do all they can for you, so don't assume that they are going to criticise or disapprove of you! Don't be afraid to be pleasantly persistent if information or help is not forthcoming.

- **Be as informed as possible about your child's particular needs**. The more you know, the more you can do to help. Through doctors, books, support organisations, even the Internet, you can gain much useful information, even if you are not medical or scientific in any way. Then you will be much better prepared to discuss diagnoses, prognoses and possible treatments with the experts and will better understand their explanations (even if you do have to rush to your books afterwards!). A word of warning about the Internet: though it does have much of great value on it, there is also a lot of unsubstantiated rubbish as well, with people claiming cures and remedies without any backing at all. So be judicious in your use of this informational tool!

- **Ensure that your other children are not missing out**. This is always a danger if one child requires and often demands a great deal of attention. Try and make time for them without their sibling. They too must be able to express their feelings about the situation without being made to feel guilty or deficient. Don't show shock if they sometimes speak bluntly about their feelings regarding their brother or sister, but encourage them to get things in perspective and pray with them about it. Give your other children lots of appreciation and lots of fun. If you have to spend a lot of time with the one child, for instance on hospital visits or stays, make sure that the others have a positive alternative with exciting babysitters!

- **Don't feel guilty!** Perhaps more than others, parents of children with special needs can be plagued with guilt. Subconsciously, they wonder whether they were somehow responsible for what has happened to their child. Or they worry that they are not doing enough for him. Or they feel guilty because sometimes they feel angry or resentful towards this child who should invite only feelings of love and compassion. If you feel like that, attempt to stop immediately! Guilt is not from God and should therefore be banished. True wrongdoing can be forgiven, and the rest is falsehood and must be thrown out! Instead, try consciously to be thankful for all the good things about your life, all the things that you are doing well, all the love and laughter you give and receive.

- **Keep your relationship with God fresh**. This is not a simple matter when you are exhausted or frustrated. It might even feel as if God should never have allowed this to happen to you and your child. Rather than sideline him, though, it helps to take all these feelings to him and talk it through with him. If you can, allow yourself time to sit in his presence and worship him. As previously suggested, a tape is often useful, especially if it has been some time since you have been able to do this. As you relax and become aware of his presence, then you are open to experience his wonderful healing and restoring touch, and you will be filled with the 'inexpressible joy' which is not dependent on circumstances. At these times, the Lord will often speak to you about your child, and give you insight and wisdom for the future. Pray for your child and ask for healing, but don't get 'hung up' on it. The Lord heals in many and mysterious ways – but that is another book entirely! Instead, concentrate on bringing God's presence and his principles into your everyday life with your child. As he gets to know the Lord for himself, there will be a gradual transformation as miraculous as any healing.

A unique individual

I've been mothered, smothered, cuddled, kissed,
then moved from pillar to post,
there's a game I'll swear everyone plays,
to see who can help me the most.

I'm kept in the dark about ordinary things
that everybody knows.
It's love without the heart for it,
and they don't think it shows.

This is me, the me you see, it's really all I've got.
I'd like someone to tell me
I'd like someone to tell me
am I beautiful, am I beautiful, am I beautiful
or what?

This is not the way I imagined they would care,
whispered conversations,
curious stares
I'm no experiment and I'm not a fragile doll.
it's a wonder I'm here at all.

And I'd like someone to tell me
I'd like someone to tell me . . .
Look me in the eye and say it, say you love me
just the way I am.

(Adrian Snell, Phil Thomson, *Beautiful . . . or What?!*, Word
UK Ltd, 1993)

The essential, eternal value of a child with special needs is no different from anyone else's. We, with our finite minds and perceptions might view him as distinct, even unintentionally treat him as inferior, but to the Lord he is precious just as he is. *'The Lord does not look at the things that man looks at. Man looks at the outward appearance, but the Lord looks at the heart'* (1 Samuel 16:7). As humans, we are too quick to judge by externals, to measure success or failure by society's norms. Adrian Snell, in the introduction to his album, *Beautiful . . . or What?!*, challenges all of us: 'Who would dare to define what is normal, and who fits the definition? After all, none of us are without a handicap of some sort.' People on the margins of our 'norms' confront us with the necessity to review our values and look again at what is really important.

Writer Mark Stewart-Jones tells movingly of how his daughter, Sophie, expressed her individuality to those around her. She suffers from cerebral palsy, and is severely restricted in what she can do physically. She spent all of her infanthood being nurtured and stimulated by her parents, particularly her father, who remained at home to care for her. Every day, they would spend an hour or two in front of the word processor, which fascinated her. When she was old enough for full-time school, Mark realised that it would be difficult to convey the full extent of her abilities to those who would be assessing her: 'While I remained confident of her intelligence I was becoming increasingly aware that I needed a means of proving this. There had always been something, an awareness I glimpsed in her eyes, but it was too abstract to construct a particularly persuasive report around.'

In the end, though, Sophie herself showed that she was able to express that intelligence. With help to hold the pencil and move the paper, she was able to write at the age of five. All those hours of watching words on a screen had taught her that there is more than one way to communicate, and she has been communicating through the written word ever since. Mark makes a profound comment on the experience: 'I mistrust a happy ending: it can often blind us to the unconditional nature of love. But I didn't spend those five years stimulating her because I refused to accept her condition. On the contrary, I did it precisely because my acceptance was so complete' (*The Independent on Sunday*, 18 January 1998).

The Lord's ways are higher than ours, and those with 'disabilities' are often the quickest to perceive the essence of those ways. Each child with learning or physical difficulties is an individual, unique and beautiful to God. He sees from the inside out, not the other way round, and while he has compassion for the problems in that child's life, he also loves him as he is now, not as he might or should become. Bringing up a child who does not respond or behave as we would expect, who does not express himself in appropriate or comprehensible ways and whose progress towards independence is a faltering struggle, is a tremendous challenge and very hard work. There needs to be reality rather than sentimentality in our approach, so that parents can admit to their own needs without feeling guilty. But do not think that your hopes and dreams for this child are over, or unbearably limited. He has the potential for amazing exploits in body, mind, and most of all, spirit.

12

Perfect Parenting?

But I have raised you up for this very purpose, that I might show you my power and that my name might be proclaimed in all the earth.
Exodus 9:16

They were a young couple, on the threshold of their life together. They did not have much money, for he was a manual worker and she did not have paid employment. They were not intellectual; their education was limited, though they did not lack intelligence. But they loved God, and were motivated by a desire to serve him and live according to his ways. They could not have argued a theological treatise, but they knew how to worship the living God. And the Lord used these characteristics in the young couple to change the history of the world and bring it back in line with his purposes.

You might think that Mary and Joseph had an unfair advantage. Parenting a perfect child must surely be an easier job than the rest of us have. In fact, they must surely have been near-perfect parents! So there is no point in using them as an example, because they did not really know what true parenting was like. Conversely, though, one could argue that as God chose them to parent his son, then they must be his ideal family, upon which we can model ourselves. Though their experience differed from ours in several significant areas, they also knew the joys and anxieties that every parent knows, and their lives highlight some valuable parenting principles. As we look to Jesus in every area of our lives, so let us learn from his family life in an effort to improve our parenting.

Both Mary and Joseph were completely submitted to God. His plans for them were not an easy option, touching as they did on the most intimate area of their relationship. The implications for Mary were painful. She literally had to offer up her body to the Lord, and then suffer the shame of an unmarried pregnancy, knowing that no one would believe her explanations. Yet her reply to God's messenger was unequivocal; *'I am the Lord's servant . . . May it be to me as you have said'* (Luke 1:38). When the Lord confirmed his words to her through her cousin Elizabeth, her immediate response was not to get into a good gossip about the situation, or bewail the circumstances, but to worship God. Her poem of praise, one of the most well known in the world, is moving in its joy and its appreciation of God's greatness. She had God's perspective on her life.

Joseph, too, though less of a high-profile character, was a man who loved God and was willing to follow him, no matter what the cost. When he first found out that Mary was pregnant, and knowing that he was not the father, he felt that he had no alternative but to terminate the relationship. But because he was *'a righteous man, and did not want to expose her to public disgrace, he had in mind to divorce her quietly'* (Matthew 1:19). The dream in which God spoke to him changed his mind completely. Instead of dismissing the dream as the product of an overheated imagination, he identified the presence of God in it, and believed the words he had heard concerning Mary and the unborn child. That was a brave act of faith, undertaken because he was a man who knew God, and so recognised these unlikely events as being from him. We are told that *'when Joseph woke up, he did what the angel of the Lord commanded him and took Mary home as his wife. But he had no union with her until she gave birth to a son'* (Matthew 1:24–5). Joseph understood the seriousness of what he was involved in, and remained completely obedient to the Lord, even though it must have been very difficult at times.

To make the most of the power available to us as parents, we also need to be totally surrendered to the Lord. Believing and acting upon his words for our lives is something we assent to in theory, but find more difficult to put into practice. How good it is that there is always opportunity for fresh resolve to seek God's forgiveness and help for the future. As we ask him to

> *Search me, O God, and know my heart,*
> *test me and know my anxious thoughts,*
> *See if there is any offensive way in me,*
> *and lead me in the way everlasting.*
>
> (Psalm 139:23–4)

he will respond, dealing gently but firmly with those anxious thoughts and offensive ways, but then helping us to start again, keeping our focus on him.

Mary and Joseph kept a sense of destiny about their son. They never forgot the purposes that God had for him. When Jesus was born, many people prophesied over him, and his parents *'marvelled'*, *'treasured up all these things and pondered them'*, and then kept them alive in their memories (Luke 2:33, 19). As the little boy grew up, he would have become aware for himself of a sense of destiny, but this would have been developed and nurtured by his godly parents. By the time he was twelve, he knew that he *'had to be in [his] Father's house'* (Luke 2:49) and though Mary and Joseph did not really understand exactly what he meant, it is obvious that he had been well schooled in the ways of God, ready for such a moment.

We also should maintain an overview of God's destiny for our children. We may not know exactly what form it will take, but we should prepare them as best we can for what God has in store for them. As has been discussed earlier, parenting is essentially a long-term project. Although we often feel that we are bogged down in our immediate circumstances, and think we can only take decisions for the next stage ahead, in reality we are investing in the future. This, though it sounds scary, can be a real release, as it helps to keep things in perspective, and remind us again of how dependent upon the Lord we are.

In many ways, Jesus was an ordinary child, requiring practical, emotional and spiritual care. As the carol says, 'He was little, weak and helpless / Tears and smiles like us he knew.' He was as much prone to childish irresponsibility as our own little darlings, but, (unlike our own little darlings!) his attitude was always righteous. I'm sure that when he was small he wrought the usual toddler havoc wherever he went, and needed as much attention during potty training as the next child. But he did not go through the 'terrible twos', because he did not have any rebelliousness in him. Even when he was older, he still behaved in a childlike way, rather than as a premature adult. Mary and Joseph spent three days feverishly searching for him among the pilgrims thronging Jerusalem for the Passover. Every parent will identify with the rising panic as realisation dawns that he is not where you thought he was. They finally found him in the Temple and Mary challenged him, as any parent would. He was irresponsible not to have mentioned where he was going. It was not a sin, though, but a symptom of his childishness. He had assumed that they would know where he was, presumably because they had so encouraged him in pursuing his godly destiny. Jesus explained this to them and then went with them and '*was obedient to them*' (Luke 2:51).

The Bible is at pains to point out that Jesus grew up as a normal human child, the embodiment of God's plan for children. He developed physically, mentally, emotionally and spiritually just as God always intended for all children; '*Jesus grew in wisdom and in stature, and in favour with God and men*' (Luke 2:52). To have achieved such development meant that his parents worked hard at their God-given task of caring for him.

Throughout Jesus's life, we see evidence of the close bond between him and his mother (Joseph, it is believed, died quite early) and at his death, in all the agony of his suffering, he still looked out for Mary's interests, charging John to look after her.

It is no accident that the birth and early life of Jesus are recorded in the Bible. It was partly to demonstrate more fully his humanity, but also to emphasise the significance God places on family life. If Jesus, son of the mighty God, Saviour of humankind, could live in an ordinary family and undergo all the normal experiences of childhood, then that transforms the status of the family and the possibilities of our own parenting. Though our children will never be perfect as Jesus was, yet it is possible for them too to grow strong, to be filled with wisdom and for the grace of God to be on them (Luke 2:40). The power of God, channelled through us, will assure the process. God can use us in our parenting, as he used Mary and Joseph, to an extent greater than we ever dreamed possible.

Preconceived parenting!

No, this is not some new type of family planning scheme, but a reference to all the preconceptions we carry into parenthood. Some of these are obtained in our childhood, so that we either think that everything should be done the way that our parents did it, or that nothing should. Other preconceptions come from the idealised portrayal of family life promoted by advertising. The perfect family should have smiling, smartly dressed children happily playing with their toys or travelling somewhere exciting in the back of very safe cars, while the perfect parents spend hours of quality time improving their children's minds and bodies, as well as cooking them enormous, healthy meals and taking them on tension-free holidays. Then, all the childcare manuals and ante-natal information we accumulate create yet more preconceptions. There seems to be a 'right' way of doing things (which varies according to what we read!) and we strive towards those right ways, anxious not to fail at this important job.

> My mother really was the perfect mother. She told me that she was only going to have one child, so that she could bring it up properly . . . All my food was home-made, and she read to me every night, and played with me. She never lost her temper, never. When I was naughty, she would sit down and explain to me why my behaviour was antisocial and its possible negative consequences . . . I was constantly occupied, and I learnt to read when I was three. Even when I wasn't at school, my life was timetabled . . . When I was a child, I was very proud of my mother . . . I was allowed out when I was a teenager. She never stopped me meeting boys. She wasn't a restrictive mother; she was the perfect mother.

So speaks Jasmin, in Sherry Ashworth's novel *The Perfect Mother* (Signet, 1994), depicting the type of parent that at first glance we might all aspire to become. The type of parent, in fact, that makes the rest of us feel hopelessly inadequate. In our different ways, sometimes without even realising it, we all aim for this preconceived perfection in our parenting, and berate ourselves when we do not achieve it. The novel, however, in exploring the concept of perfect motherhood and the different ideals we all have, inevitably reaches the verdict that there is no such thing. Jasmin in adulthood rejects her mother, acknowledging that she is being stifled by her, and the book concludes that even 'the perfect mother has imperfections'.

And there is nothing like writing a book on parenting to highlight those imperfections! (Not that I ever set myself up as the 'perfect mother'!) Whenever I have been away from it, this book has returned to plague me! In the very act of speaking crossly to one of the children, my own words float mockingly through my brain, accompanied by others, such as 'hypocrite'.

I interrupt one child to tell another one off and a whole chunk of Chapter 6 reverberates in my mind! The book has taken a long time to write, partly because every paragraph has been sweated over, and partly because the irony of shutting myself away from the children to write a book on parenting was too much for me to cope with! Every issue that I have addressed on paper has confronted me in reality during the time of writing. I have been forced to line the theory up with the practice, a valuable but sometimes painful process.

Possessing the vision

Despite this, I have a passionate belief in the ability we all have, with God's help, to do a good job as parents. I have a vision of families growing up in the ways of God, loving him, others and themselves. Of a Church which grows because its families are demonstrating the power of God in their lives and are reaching out to others to share this power. Of a society transformed because a generation of children are growing up secure, happy and cared for. Of parents enjoying their children because they no longer feel dragged down by guilt and anger. Is such a vision a possibility, or the product of a naive triumphalism? Faced with the realities of family life in the 1990s, the soaring divorce rate, the increasing abuse of children, the chaotic, disrupted lifestyles so many children are forced to live, and the difficulties we ourselves often have with our own parenting, we might conclude that such ideas are an irrelevant fantasy.

Yet *'with man, this is impossible, but not with God; all things are possible with God'* (Mark 10:27). We have to be able to aim for his best, even though, to our natural minds, it seems an unattainable dream. Knowing what God's ideals are for our parenting and asking his help to achieve them is not the same as perfectionism. For in the latter we are relying on our own resources, whereas in the former we are availing ourselves of his power and his compassion. God is more forgiving and accepting of our shortcomings than we are! We cannot be perfect parents, but it is still vital to keep hold of an overall vision of where we are going. Parenthood is an act of faith, both in the everyday ups and downs, and in the long-term goals.

The respondents to my questionnaire reflected this need to maintain a wider view of parenthood. One of them wrote, 'Childhood is magic. Give children a well-balanced childhood and hopefully they will grow into well-balanced adults and parents.' Another participant made the observation that children are in some respects a mirror image of ourselves. 'As long as we are happy and spend plenty of time with them, having fun and learning, then we as parents reap the benefits of bright, happy children. It all goes towards making it a thoroughly enjoyable and memorable experience (and one to be strongly recommended!).' Many comments emphasised the long-term responsibility of parenting, not only to the children, but to the community as a whole. A mother of five summed it up thus: 'As a parent we have a responsibility at least to try and shape our children's future in a way that will benefit society as well as them as individuals. I think, somewhere along the line, that it shapes us as people too!'

It is perhaps good, every now and then, for parents to step back from their immediate circumstances and review their parenting as a whole. Several of the respondents in the questionnaire remarked on how helpful it had been to think more deeply about aspects of parenthood that they would not normally consider. Obviously, too much 'navel-gazing' is not wise or healthy, but the occasional assessment and targeting exercise can be extremely beneficial. The questionnaire is included at the back, as a possible starter for such an exercise.

Having a perception of parenting which encompasses the future does not in any way lessen the demands of the present. It is as we try to come to terms with the discrepancy between the two that we often increase our feeling of failure as parents.

The aims for our children, outlined in Chapter 1, often do not seem to be achieved when we look at our immediate circumstances. However, I firmly believe that we have to have faith that, as Doug Horley puts it, 'step by step we are moving forward, little by little we are gaining ground' ('We want to see Jesus lifted high', Kingsway's Thank You Music, 1993). Parenting does not deliver instant results; it is an investment over years, requiring patience and determination, but also giving wonderful returns along the way!

Power for the taking!

No, we are not going to be perfect parents, but we *can* be powerful parents, empowered by the Lord, who gives all the resources we need. One of the purposes of this book is to encourage parents that with the Lord they have all they need, and that he really does give us power to parent well. There is no need for us to feel guilty about our failures; with God's help, we can put them right and have a fresh start.

Describing his ministry, Paul declared that he would not let himself be discouraged, and did not rely on his own natural strength: *'We have this treasure in jars of clay, to show that this all-surpassing power is from God and not from us. We are hard pressed on every side, but not crushed; perplexed but not in despair, persecuted, but not abandoned, struck down, but not destroyed'* (2 Corinthians 4:7–9). Of course, circumstances are not usually as dire as described here, but they can sometimes feel like it! The point is that the power we need in our everyday lives is indeed from God and not from us. The responsibility of parenthood is not our responsibility after all. Delegated, yes, but ultimately it is the Lord's, and he does not fail. Understanding this can take a tremendous burden from us.

It is possible, with God's help, to remain in patient, wise control through all the crises and strains of family life! It is possible to keep your temper and present a fairly consistent example of God's love in action. It is possible to be fair, open, cheerful and positive, to dispense discipline in an ordered, biblical manner, to listen, encourage and forgive and to have fun in the midst of it all! Not only possible, but accessible, if we turn round our thinking and acknowledge that only God can do all that, and that our task is to stay close to the source of the power and let him work through us.

Some people might feel that they do not have the power of God in their parenting, that it is not a likely prospect for them and that these words are glib and irrelevant. I can identify with the view; we all have times when we feel like that. But I would urge you not to give up on the idea. Take your feelings back to the Lord, as suggested in Chapter 4, and *'be still and know that [he is] God'* (Psalm 46:10). Spending time with God, becoming increasingly aware of his love, his might and his wisdom, worshipping him and talking to him is the best way to avail ourselves of the power he offers. This is confirmed in Isaiah, who encourages us to take heart and trust the Lord:

Do you not know? Have you not heard?
The LORD is the everlasting God, the creator of the ends of the earth.
He will not grow tired or weary, and his understanding no one can
fathom.
He gives strength to the weary and increases the power of the weak.
Even youths grow tired and weary, and young men stumble and
fall,
but those who hope in the LORD will renew their strength.
They will soar on wings like eagles; they will run and not grow
weary,
they will walk and not be faint. (Isaiah 40:28–31)

That is God's promise to us; that he will renew our strength. The image of the eagle is a beautiful one, conveying a sense of freedom, exhilaration and power. We can increasingly attain to all those characteristics in our parenting as we focus our hope and confidence on the Lord.

Pleasure, not pressure!

'Mum, do you like having children?' asked one of my sons the other day. The question did not come after some confrontation or domestic eruption, so I assumed that it was academic rather than insecure!

'What makes you ask?' I replied, thinking that, nonetheless, I needed a clearer context for the question.

'Well, I just wondered, 'cos it does seem like hard work, and I was wondering whether to have any myself.'

Well, it *is* hard work, particularly with a large family, but my answer to him was an unhesitating yes! I love having children, and he couldn't do better with his life than go on to be a good father himself. The joys and pleasures of being a parent far outweigh the demands and pressures. The depths of feeling aroused in us for and about our children are incredible, and add immeasurably to the quality of our essential being. We glimpse the parent heart of God in our own responses to our children, and learn more of him as we continue in our parenting. Parenthood is a deeply spiritual experience, which also incorporates fun, happiness and friendship.

Having children, as Sheila Kitzinger states, means 'to take on one of the most emotionally and intellectually demanding, exasperating, strenuous, anxiety arousing and deeply satisfying tasks that any human being can undertake' (*Ourselves as Mothers*, Doubleday, 1992). The pressures are undeniable and Christians are in no way immune to them. Indeed, they have more, in some ways, because they are parenting against the flow of our culture. While I do not have slick answers, and fail frequently, I do have a burning desire to encourage myself and other parents in the godly principles and practicalities of family life, for it is my firm conviction that the Lord holds the blueprint for successful parenting, and that we miss the best if we do not follow it.

The time children spend in our care is comparatively short, and we need to make the most of it. Before we know it, the years have slipped away, and our babies are ready to make their own way in the world. Our influence, whether for good or bad, is stronger than we probably realise as we muddle through their childhood. The input we have when they are young will have lasting significance, and relationships forged with them in their early years will endure for ever. So it is crucial to ensure that our priorities are right in this 'window of opportunity'!

Surrounding them with love and security, helping them to develop self-discipline, responsibility and a caring attitude, encouraging them to discover themselves and God and to fulfil their potential in every area of their lives are all vital elements in our parenting job description. So are creating happy memories of fun and laughter, of silly moments, exciting activities and family traditions. Being a parent certainly is one of the most important jobs on earth, and *you* are uniquely qualified to undertake it. The job specification comes from God, and he makes sure that you are '*thoroughly equipped for every good work*' (2 Timothy 3:17) by giving you the power to make it a fulfilling, enjoyable success. Parent power is a reality, with the purpose of transforming lives: our children's, our own, and those of the of the community in which we live.

Power to parent is not the power of positive thinking, which runs out of steam very rapidly, but an endlessly renewable resource, supplied by a loving Father, to give us the very best in our family life. As with so many aspects of parenting, it is a paradox; the more it is used, the more there is available. As you continue in this extraordinary, life-shaping work, '*I pray that out of his glorious riches [God] may strengthen you with power through his Spirit in your inner being, so that Christ may dwell in your hearts through faith*' (Ephesians 3:16–17).

Useful Resources

Books

Sherry Ashworth, *The Perfect Mother* (Penguin, 1994)

Janet Balaskas, *Active Birth* (Unwin Paperbacks, 1983)

Sheila Bridge, *The Art of Plate Spinning* (Hodder & Stoughton, 1996)

Ross Campbell, *How to Really Love Your Children* (Inspirational Press, 1996)

Vivien Devlin, *Motherhood from 1920 to the Present Day* (Polygon, 1995)

James Dobson, *The New Dare to Discipline* (Kingsway Publications, 1993) (Any of James Dobson's books offer helpful principles and practical advice.)

David and Liz Holden, *Raising Children – a parent's privilege* (Kingsway Publications, 1995)

Penelope Leach, *Baby and Child* (Penguin Books, 1985)

David and Vera Mace, *How to have a Happy Marriage* (Abingdon, 1977)

Bob Myers, *Parenting Teenagers* (Jessica Kingsley Publishers, 1996)

Rob Parsons, *The Sixty Minute Father* (Hodder & Stoughton, 1995)

Bette M. Ross, *Our Special Child* (Nelson Word, 1994)

Joni Eareckson Tada, *All God's Children* (Marshall Pickering, 1992)

Video

Bartholomew: How a Christian family came to see their severely handicapped child as a gift from God (S. P. Valley, code VC007)

Organisations

British Agencies for Adoption and Fostering (BAAF)
Skyline House
200, Union Street
London SW1 0LX
Information and a publications catalogue with some excellent books can be obtained from the above.

Care for the Family
Garth House
Leon Avenue
Cardiff CF4 7RG
Tel: 01222 810800
Excellent seminars, videos and publications to support the family.

Marriage Resource
24, West Street
Wimborne
Dorset BH21 1JS
Tel: 01202 849000
Information about marriage enhancement and counselling.

Parental Network for the Post-Institutionalised Child
31, Court Lane
Wolstanton
Newcastle
Staffs ST5 8DE

Tel: 01782 858915
Support and information for adoptive parents of institution-
  alised children.

Rapport, part of *Care for the Family*
Garth House
Leon Avenue
Cardiff CF4 7RG
Communication workshops, conflict management, marriage
  enrichment in every area.

Citizens Advice Bureau has information on other support
  organisations and resources not mentioned here.

Parenting Questionnaire

This is the questionnaire Sue used to gain an insight into how a selection of parents viewed every aspect of parenting. It is included here as an aid for you to review your parenting as a whole. The questions may seem a little random, but they are designed specifically to fit into the structure of the book.

Number of children: .... Names & ....
Ages: ....
....
....

What factors influenced your choice of family size?
....
....
....

What are your general aims for your children?
....
....
....
....

What do you find the most rewarding aspects of parenting?
....
....
....

What do you find the most demanding aspect of parenting?

....

....

....

What would you say were the two most over-riding emotions of parenthood?

....

....

....

What things do you feel guilty about in your parenting?

....

....

....

Which child, if any, have you found most easy to parent? Can you say why?

....

....

....

What are your methods of discipline?

....

....

....

What, if any, are your religious/spiritual beliefs?

....

....

....

In what ways do these beliefs affect your parenting?

....

....

....